AUDITING AT THE SPEED OF RISK WITH AN AGILE, *CONTINUOUS* AUDIT PLAN

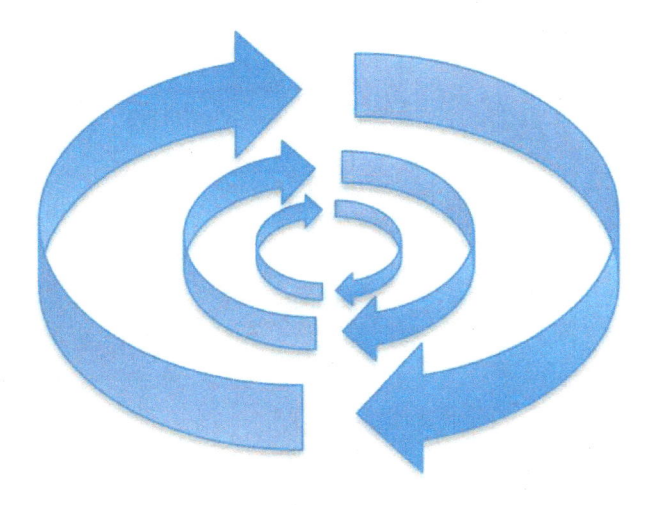

Norman D. Marks, CPA, CRMA

© Norman Marks, 2021, all rights reserved

Auditing at the Speed of Risk with an Agile, Continuous Audit Plan

Contents

Acknowledgments 7

My Continuous Audit Plan Journey 9

Introduction 15

1. **Why do we need an Audit Plan?** 21
   Why an annual plan? _____ 23

2. **The Audit Committee** 25

3. **Defining the Budget and necessary Resources** 29
   A Dynamic Audit Plan _____ 30
   When the Budget may not be Sufficient _____ 37
   Defining the Resources _____ 46

4. **IT Audit Planning** 51

5. **Risk Assessment** 53
   IIA Guidance _____ 53
      Standard 2010 53
      Standard 2201 and 2210 56
      IIA UK Guidance 59
   Auditing what matters _____ 60
   It starts with enterprise objectives _____ 61
   Reliance on management's risk assessment _____ 62
   When there is no management risk assessment, audit it __ 65
   When there is a risk management activity _____ 68
   If there is nothing by management, do it yourself _____ 69
      Interviewing the executives 71
      Auditing by Walking Around 77
      Gathering the views of the internal audit team 77
      Discussions with the Audit Committee 78
   It's not just about the downside of risk _____ 80
      The 'risk' of losing opportunities 80
      Value-based auditing 82

© Norman Marks, 2022, all rights reserved   3

IT-related sources of risk	87
Third and Fourth Party Risk	92
Governance and Organizational Culture	94

6. The Universe 99

7. Which audits should we perform?................................101

Focus, Focus, and Agility	101
Choices in Audit Strategy	103
Assurance or Consulting?	110
Reliance on other Assurance Providers	113
Outsourcing	116
Other Types of Audit Project	117
Software Project	117
Control Self-Assessment	118
Audits of Third Parties	120
Investigations	122
Assistance to the External Auditor	123
Internal Audit's role in Sarbanes-Oxley Compliance	124
Summary	124

8. What is in the Audit Plan? 127

Review of the Prior Year	128
Audit Strategy	129
Strategic Plan?	129
What will we Audit?	130

9. Communicating the Audit Plan 131

The Internal Review	131
The Review with Management	132
The Review with the External Auditor	134
The Review with the Audit Committee	134

10. Maintaining the Audit Plan 137

    Continuous Risk Assessment _____ 137

    The Rolling Audit Plan _____ 138
        Continuous risk management 140
        Continuous conversations 140
        Continuous monitoring 145

    Changing and communicating the rolling audit plan _____ 146
        Working with top management and the Audit Committee 147

    Continuous audit planning and the annual audit plan_____ 149

Closing Thoughts 151

Appendix I: Solectron Audit Strategy 157

Appendix II: Tosco Audit Plan 163

Appendix III: Business Objects Audit Plan 177

About the Author 187

Acknowledgments

I have been honored to have a review panel of esteemed practitioners and experts.

Each has provided constructive feedback to a draft of this book, adding huge value for which I am very grateful.

- Doug Anderson, retired CAE at Dow Chemical; formerly the Vice Chair of the Institute of Internal Auditors (IIA) for Professional Guidance; and a member of the IIA's American Hall of Distinguished Practitioners.

- Professor Andrew Chambers, who has served as chair of the audit committee of a UK financial institution; professor of internal auditing and corporate governance; director of the (UK) Institute of Internal Auditors Inc; the recipient of multiple awards from the IIA; a member of their International Standards Board; and the author of more than two dozen books

- John Fraser, retired Senior Vice President, Internal Audit and Chief Risk Officer of Hydro One Networks Inc; author of *Enterprise Risk Management*; and recipient of the Canadian Institute of Internal Auditors' Lifetime Achievement Award

- Steve Goepfert, retired Vice President, Internal Audit at United Airlines; past Chairman of the IIA; recipient of the IIA's Victor Z. Brink Award for Distinguished Service; and inducted into the IIA's American Hall of Distinguished Practitioners

- Larry Harrington, retired Vice President, Internal Audit at Raytheon Corporation; past Chairman of the IIA; and recipient of the IIA's Victor Z. Brink Award for Distinguished Service

- Bob McDonald, retired Chief Governance Officer, head of internal audit and risk at Queensland Health; former chair of the Audit and Risk Committee of the Queensland Department of National Parks, Recreation, Sport and Racing; past Chairman of the IIA; and recipient of the IIA's Victor Z. Brink Award for Distinguished Service

- N. G. Shankar, retired Group Executive Vice President – Corporate Audit at Aditya Birla Group; former member of the Board of the IIA; and author of a handbook on internal audit for company directors and executive management published by the Institute of Internal Auditors, India

- Paul Sobel, retired CAE at Georgia-Pacific; former Chairman of the IIA; Chairman of COSO; recipient of the IIA's Victor Z. Brink Award for Distinguished Service; author of "Managing Risks in Uncertain Times: Leveraging COSO'S New ERM Framework" and other books; and President of the Internal Audit Foundation

Each of the review panel members commented on drafts of this book, but they have different experiences and there are topics where we have taken different paths. For example, Doug Anderson believes that investigations are not an internal audit function but should be handled by management. He considers it a "second line" responsibility. My approach, which I believe he accepts, is that any responsibility outside traditional internal auditing should be discussed with and approved by the Audit Committee of the board.

I am pleased that they all consider this book of value to both experienced and new internal audit executives. I am grateful also that they have given me permission to quote them a few times.

I also want to express my appreciation for the support of my team members at each of my companies, as well as the board members and senior executives who gave me the freedom to innovate.

My Continuous Audit Plan Journey

We need to stop auditing the past and turn towards auditing what matters today and will matter in the future.

I was a chief audit executive (CAE) with major companies, most of which were global, for a couple of decades.

Each of my companies was different, and each had its own challenges.

My first opportunity as CAE was with *Tosco Corporation*. I joined after an investor group took control but were unable to sell the company and decided to run it themselves. I was one of their first hires.

The entire internal audit team had left so I was able to bring on my own people and adopt what I believed was the best approach for the company. I had ten years of public accounting experience and several years as a direct report to excellent CAEs at previous organizations, but I was still learning.

I was lucky to have an Audit Committee that was extremely supportive and an extraordinary management team. The CEO[1] was brilliant and his leadership of Tosco literally changed the oil refinery business. He was supported by a first-rate CFO and first-class executives in the company's two divisions.

Over my more than ten years with Tosco as CAE, my team grew nearly as fast as the company (which went from $2bn in revenue and marginal net income to a highly profitable $28bn company). It started small with three people and grew to twenty-eight internal auditors,

---

[1] The CEO was Tom O'Malley, who was profiled in 1997 by *Forbes*. The article can be found at
https://www.forbes.com/forbes/1997/0113/5901104a.html?sh=53ef371744c0

fifty when you include specialists in contract auditing, investigations, contingency planning, and IT quality assurance.

The methodology I developed over time at Tosco is the foundation for the thinking in this book. However, each of the companies I worked at after Tosco was different. Each therefore required modification to the audit strategy and methodology, although the fundamental principles remained the same:

1. Provide the Audit Committee and management with the *assurance*, *advice*, and *insight* they need *on what matters now and will matter in the future*[2] to the success of the business.
2. Provide the *actionable* information they need *when* they need it.
3. Be *agile* and *efficient* in both planning and execution of every audit engagement.
4. *Focus* on what matters and exclude from scope anything that does not matter.
5. Write (and otherwise communicate) for the time-limited, speed-reading executive. Don't waste anybody's time but get the message across and drive action!
6. Work *with* management[3] to ensure they can rely on their processes, systems, organization, and controls as they direct and manage the company to achieve its objectives.
7. Measure the success of internal audit by the success of the company, not by the number of audits performed or the number of issues identified.
8. Recognize that quality and effectiveness are best recognized through the eyes of the satisfied customer[4].

---

[2] As best we can
[3] Richard Chambers refers to this as being a *Trusted Advisor*.
[4] Primarily the Audit Committee of the board, while recognizing the need to add value to executive and other members of management.

I left Tosco when it was acquired by a much larger company. The next company was a totally different proposition.

Solectron Corporation had been a highly regarded, entrepreneurial company that dominated its space. It had grown rapidly through acquisition and the CEO, CFO, and the Audit Committee all welcomed me on board as CAE.

However, I joined as CAE of an established internal audit function just as its fortunes were about to turn. Not only was the CFO that had recruited me pushed to the side (she left soon after) and replaced by a less than supportive individual[5], but the CEO was himself replaced within a matter of months.

The culture at the company was unhealthy, with the top executives competing[6] instead of working as a team. (In time, this and other management failings led to the company losing market share and being sold to a competitor after I left.)

As I will explain in the text, the company had over a hundred manufacturing and assembly plants scattered around the world. They operated independently rather than as an integrated network. For example, each had their own CIO who, with the accounting staff, reported to operating management rather than to the corporate finance or IT teams.

With such a diversified operation and a staff of about fifteen, the methods I used with success at Tosco had to change. I designed and implemented a novel approach that relied on control-self assessments and focused audits (which I will detail).

After Solectron, I joined *Maxtor Corporation*. It was the global leader in hard drive manufacturing, both in terms of revenue and technology. At $4bn in revenue, it was smaller than either Tosco or Solectron.

---

[5] I found out later that the new CFO had been hired before I was offered a position, but it was kept a secret. This was not a good sign! The new CFO did not want me to report to the Audit Committee, informing me that I worked for him and only him. Our relationship was never constructive.
[6] They even bid against each other for a customer's business.

Maxtor had different problems that eventually led to its demise as an independent company. It had made a poor decision some years earlier, setting up a plant in Northern California to manufacture an essential component in every hard drive while its competitors manufactured that component in Asia. The difference in cost was an insurmountable burden in designing cost-effective, next-generation products.

The company had multiple material weaknesses in its system of internal control over financial reporting (i.e., Sarbanes-Oxley or "SOX" compliance). It relied on KPMG for both its internal audit function and the design and execution of its SOX compliance program.

I insourced both internal audit and the SOX compliance program, adapting my methodology to suit. Fixing the company's financial reporting processes and controls was a top priority for the Audit Committee. But that had to be balanced by the need to address the other significant sources of risk to the company. I supported the company's plans to build a new factory in Thailand[7] to replace the Northern California one, but it was too late.

When Maxtor was sold, I joined *Business Objects S.A.* It was even smaller but highly profitable (which I appreciated) and the leader in the business analytics space. There was an existing internal audit team, but it lacked IT audit resources – which I quickly added. With management and board approval, I also added SOX compliance to my portfolio.

I needed to change my approach again as with Business Objects the three greatest sources of risk were revenue, revenue, and revenue. The company had only recently suffered from a long and intrusive investigation into revenue-related fraud, primarily in Asia.

The approach I adopted, which is illustrated by the audit plan included in the book, remained true to the principles listed above. I was fortunate to hire an excellent team that delivered quality and timely results.

---

[7] This is where most of our competitors had built plants and the country had a reliable infrastructure and labor force.

Business Objects was my last CAE position, but I have continued to develop my thinking in my semi-retirement.

The concepts and practices discussed in this book reflect my experience. They helped me deliver what my customers on the Audit Committee and in management told me that they valued. I will return to those principles at the end of the book.

Every CAE needs to adopt practices and methodologies that are *tailored* to their organization and the expectations of the Audit Committee of the board[8].

While I recognize that what I found worked for me and my companies may not be ideal for every organization, I believe the underlying principles should be given strong consideration by every CAE.

I hope the extensive stories and examples in the book will help every organization achieve world-class internal auditing.

---

[8] Sometimes, the expectations of the Audit Committee (as well as management) fall below what internal audit's potential. The CAE should see this as an opportunity to explain that potential and then demonstrate its value through performance.

"Audit planning and risk assessment is critical to adding value and building the internal audit brand for creating positive change. Proper risk assessment and audit planning is the most important function of the CAE, followed by hiring, training, and developing the right people to execute the plan."

> Larry Harrington, CAE at Raytheon Technologies

Introduction

> What is *internal auditing that matters*?
>
> It's an internal audit function whose *performance matters* to key stakeholders on the board and in top management.
>
> It's an internal audit function that provides *the assurance that those key stakeholders need*: assurance that they can rely on the organization's people, process, and systems to deliver on strategies and plans, achieve objectives, and deliver the desired level of value.
>
> That assurance extends to the controls that ensure both the creation and preservation of value – controls that optimize performance and manage risks to objectives.
>
> How is that achieved?
>
> Internal audit must *focus* its time and resources on issues (i.e., risks and related controls) that matter to the board and top management.
>
> It is not enough to say that internal audit is 'aligned' with the strategies and objectives of the organization. Internal audit's plans should be driven by those strategies and objectives, and the risks to their achievement.
>
> *"Auditing that Matters"*, Norman Marks

The audit plan[9] is at the heart of the internal audit activity in more ways than one.

---

[9] In particular, the schedule of which audits and other activities the internal audit activity will perform in the upcoming period(s)

- It is the living, dynamic organ that provides continuous energy and purpose.
- It determines the work that internal audit will perform.
- When you know what work will be performed, you can make sure you have the resources to do it. It drives both staffing and training plans.
- It requires constant attention and care.
- When it is not as healthy as it should be, the entire function suffers.

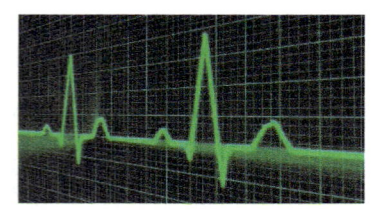

While *Auditing that Matters,* my seminal book on internal auditing published in 2016, covers building and maintaining the audit plan in some depth, I believe the audit plan is so important that it deserves a book of its own.

This book emphasizes, explains, and gives practical guidance for moving to *agile* and *continuous* audit planning, including *continuous* risk assessment, so that we are always:

Auditing what matters to the business now and will matter in the future
and
Auditing at the speed of business and its risks.

When I talk about *agile*, I am not referring to the Agile methodology that is used in software development and some have tried to adapt for internal auditing. I am talking about the *agility* of the internal audit function, its ability to react with great flexibility in an environment where the business and its environment, including risks and opportunities, are changing at speed.

By *continuous*, I am not referring to 'continuous auditing'. In fact, continuous audit planning is almost the opposite of continuous auditing! With continuous auditing, you audit the same source of risk on a frequent if not continuous basis. But with continuous audit *planning*, you audit whichever area is currently the more significant source of risk.

A continuous audit is only justified in my approach when the area *consistently* meets two criteria: (a) it is a source of significant risk, and (b) there is significant value to the organization in an audit. By that, I mean that even though it was audited last year (and possibly earlier this year), the level of risk and the value of another audit remains high.

At Tosco, I audited derivatives trading at least once each year (sometimes more frequently) because it met both criteria. But while some internal audit functions set up continuous auditing of areas like accounts payable, I did not. It might be a high-risk area every so often, but not every year.

Progress has been made in the profession over the last decade or so. Improvements include:

- The recognition that the internal audit function is not just the "eyes and ears" of the board and top management. As Richard Chambers eloquently pointed out in *Trusted Advisors: Key Attributes of Outstanding Internal Auditors* (2017), internal auditors should "provide assurance and sound advice to the board and Audit Committee". I would extend the 'customer base' to include all members of the management team throughout the extended enterprise. I would also add 'foresight and insight' to 'assurance and sound advice'.

- The development of the *Core Principles for the Professional Practice of Internal Auditing*[10] and a suggested *Mission of Internal Audit* that is:

---

[10] I was privileged to be a member of the IIA's task force that wrote the *Core Principles* and the *Mission*.

> "To enhance and protect organizational value by providing risk-based and objective assurance, advice, and insight."

Those words are critical to the value provided by internal audit to the organization. We not only protect but seek to *enhance* organizational value.

In order to do that, we not only need to focus on what matters to the organization, but also have the talent within the internal audit team to deliver high quality insight and advice that leads to any necessary action.

Our work is risk-based and extends beyond traditional audit reporting that highlights control and risk issues. It includes:

- *Assurance* that the leadership of the organization can rely on its systems, people, and processes to perform as needed for success
- *Advice* on how to improve the above, and
- The professional *insight* of the internal auditor, even if that is not included in the formal, written report to management and the board

There is a huge difference between pointing out issues (negative assurance) and indicating whether risks are being adequately managed (positive assurance). The value to our customers in being told they can rely on the organization's systems, processes, and people vs. being told of issues and being required to guess whether they can still rely, is immense.

- A broad acceptance of risk-based auditing (sometimes referred to as RBA or RBIA), where the focus of our work is on those sources of risk that could have a significant effect on the achievement of *enterprise* objectives. However, many still adhere to traditional practices (as will be discussed later) that are focused more on risks to business units and processes than the enterprise as a whole. Some refer to this as top-down auditing vs. bottoms-up auditing[11].

- The increasing number of audit teams that update their audit plans on a more continuous basis[12]. It seems that somewhere between 50% and 60% have static, annual audit plans. 30% or so update them quarterly, and 15% or more update them more than quarterly. A few still have multiple-year audit plans.

Before we can start to discuss *how* we should build the audit plan, we need to review *why* it is needed.

After all, if we want to be agile and responsive to changes in the business environment, including changes to existing risks and the emergence of new risks, why shouldn't we simply plan as we go?

---

[11] That doesn't mean there isn't a need to consider risks from the bottom up. I believe, however, that risks at a lower level of the organization should only be given priority when they could have a significant effect on the success of the organization as a whole.

[12] Both Richard Chambers in *The Speed of Risk*, 2019, and I in my books and presentations have been promoting "Auditing at the speed of risk!" for many years.

1. Why do we need an Audit Plan?

"By Failing to prepare, you are preparing to fail." Benjamin Franklin

The IIA's *International Standards for the Professional Practice of Internal Auditing*[13] require an 'audit plan' with appropriate resources:

2010 – Planning

The chief audit executive must establish a risk-based plan to determine the priorities of the internal audit activity, consistent with the organization's goals.

Interpretation:

To develop the risk-based plan, the chief audit executive consults with senior management and the board and obtains an understanding of the organization's strategies, key business objectives, associated risks, and risk management processes. The chief audit executive must review and adjust the plan, as necessary, in response to changes in the organization's business, risks, operations, programs, systems, and controls.

2010.A1 – The internal audit activity's plan of engagements must be based on a documented risk assessment, undertaken at least annually. The input of senior management and the board must be considered in this process.

2010.A2 – The chief audit executive must identify and consider the expectations of senior management, the board, and other stakeholders for internal audit opinions and other conclusions.

2010.C1[14] – The chief audit executive should consider accepting proposed consulting engagements based on

---

[13] Part of the IIA's *International Professional Practices Framework* (IPPF), last updated in 2016 and effective in 2017.
[14] There is no Standard 2010.B1.

the engagement's potential to improve management of risks, add value, and improve the organization's operations. Accepted engagements must be included in the plan.

2020 – Communication and Approval

The chief audit executive must communicate the internal audit activity's plans and resource requirements, including significant interim changes, to senior management and the board for review and approval. The chief audit executive must also communicate the impact of resource limitations.

2030 – Resource Management The chief audit executive must ensure that internal audit resources are appropriate, sufficient, and effectively deployed to achieve the approved plan.

Interpretation:

Appropriate refers to the mix of knowledge, skills, and other competencies needed to perform the plan. Sufficient refers to the quantity of resources needed to accomplish the plan. Resources are effectively deployed when they are used in a way that optimizes the achievement of the approved plan.

I will discuss each of these requirements later.

But we shouldn't do something simply because the IIA's Standards say we should. *We should do what makes sense for our business*, enabling us to provide our leaders with the assurance, advice, and insight they need.

There are valid business needs for an audit plan.

1. The Audit Committee of the board needs to see what internal audit plans to accomplish over the next period. This is essential to their oversight responsibilities.
2. The audit plan is (or at least should be) the basis for the internal audit budget for the period.

3. The plan also determines what internal and supplemental resources the function will need. In addition, the department's training plan should be tailored to deliver the capabilities needed to perform the audits in the plan with high quality.
4. Management of the internal audit function uses the plan to manage the department and its activities.

By the way, when I refer to the "audit plan" I am usually referring to the schedule of the audits and other activities that are planned. However, *audit planning* (including risk assessment and resource planning) is an essential element – and this book promotes it as a continuous activity. When the audit plan is shared with management and the board, it includes other material as explained later and shown in the attachments.

Why an annual plan?

Even though, as I will clarify shortly, internal audit needs to be agile and responsive to changes in the environment – with a *continuously* updated audit plan – there is still a need for a plan that indicates activities planned for the year.

2. The Audit Committee

"You help us sleep through the night." Charlie Luellen, Chair of the Audit Committee at Tosco Corporation

The Audit Committee of the board is charged with oversight of the internal audit function. To do that, they need to understand what the audit team will be doing over the next period.

In most organizations, the Audit Committee approves the annual audit plan. It should also approve any significant changes to that plan.

The members of the Audit Committee will normally have a broad understanding of the business and the priorities of the board. They will need to confirm that internal audit will address the issues and concerns of the whole board, not just any financial matters relevant to the Audit Committee.

They also need to gain comfort that the CAE has a broad understanding of the business, its risks, opportunities, and strategies, and will be able to provide them the assurance, advice, and insight they and top management need.

It was my practice to sit down one-on-one, face-to-face, with each member of the Audit Committee (in addition to their regular meetings and my executive sessions with them that were part of each meeting) and discuss the business, its risks, opportunities, and strategies. I wanted to tap their knowledge and experience, including their insights into what needed to go right as well as what could go wrong.

Listening to each member and taking their thoughts into consideration when building the audit plan goes a very long way to gaining not only their approval of the plan when it is presented to the Audit Committee, but their confidence in your ability to lead the audit function.

Gaining the approval of the full Audit Committee should be painless when each member has been involved in the process.

In a few organizations, management formally approves the annual plan first, but management should not be able to determine what internal audit does. It undermines their independence.

Management should be part of the process, but that process and its results are owned by internal audit.

It was my practice, and I think it is the practice of most chief internal auditors (CAEs) to solicit the input of management and listen to their thoughts (rather than their formal approval) before asking the Audit Committee for their approval. In most cases, we were able to agree.

This is not only valuable information that the CAE should consider carefully but can help gain acceptance and even support from senior management of the work internal audit will perform.

I have experienced several situations where local management questioned the reasons for an audit and more senior management gave us their valuable support.

I will come back to 'risk assessment' later.

The Audit Committee needs to understand, however, that this is not a rigid plan. It will be modified as the year progresses and as things change.

The intelligent CAE will always strive to:

- Audit *what matters* to the success of the organization
- *When it matters*
- So that its assurance, advice, and insight is *timely*, delivered when management and the board need it.

That means that the plan must be at least as dynamic as the business in understanding and responding to changes in business conditions and risks.

We need to be agile, flexing with the winds of change.

Some CAEs believe this is achieved by including an allowance for special projects and emerging risks in the audit plan. For example, they may provide a plan that lists 20 projects and a line with 20% of the budget allocated for additional audit activities[15].

But this not only infers certainty that all 20 will be performed, but also makes it hard for the CAE either to remove or even to modify those 20. It also limits the CAE's flexibility to that 20% of available resources.

In fact, the CAE needs the flexibility to modify 100% of the plan, even to the point where it exceeds the approved budget if necessary[16].

I explained to the Audit Committee that the audit plan was just that, a plan.

The plan reflects what I expect, at the present time with today's information, to accomplish over the next period. As the IIA's Core Principles for Internal Auditing say, we are forward looking. We want to audit the present and the future, not the past.

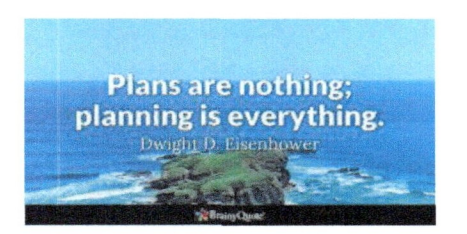

> Plans are nothing; planning is everything.
> Dwight D. Eisenhower

But:

1. I will modify it as risks or the business change.

2. I will endeavor to *audit what matters* at the time of the audit and what we can see is likely to matter in the months ahead, rather than what mattered at the time of putting together the annual plan.

3. I will inform the Audit Committee promptly if significant changes are made, seeking further approval if necessary.

---

[15] Unfortunately, some CAEs use this 20% as a way to fund overruns rather than for unplanned projects.

[16] If the risks mandate an increase in audit hours, my experience is that the Audit Committee will support a budget increase. That is not everybody's experience, but at least the CAE can ensure the Audit Committee is engaged and has a full understanding of what is left on the table.

© Norman Marks, 2022, all rights reserved

Each Audit Committee I worked with not only accepted but approved of this approach. It simply makes business sense, and they were experienced businesspeople.

There was a specific technique I used with the Audit Committee to obtain their input, which I will share in the risk assessment discussion.

3. Defining the Budget and necessary Resources

"Plans are of little importance, but planning is essential." Winston Churchill

The overriding principle is that the work that needs to be performed defines the budget and the resources that should be available to internal audit.

If you get a budget first, and then build the audit plan, you:

- May not have the resources to perform all the work that is necessary and appropriate. While you may have the number of people resources, they may not have the required skills or experience you need. This can present a challenge. Training and/or co-sourcing may be the answer, but if the problem is likely to persist, changing the composition of the audit team may be required.
- May have more resources than you need! As a result, work is performed that has little value to the board or top management – you are auditing what doesn't really matter.

While the possibility of having an excessive budget may seem unlikely, it is more common than you might believe.

Organizations may approve a budget for internal audit that is based on the previous year's budget plus an amount for inflation, or some benchmark such as internal audit costs as a percentage of revenue. If there is an acquisition, the company may simply add the internal audit budgets of the two former companies.

Any of these can result in an excessive budget, where work (including work that is not critical) is performed to fill the time available[17].

No. The budget and resourcing should flow from the audit plan, not the other way round.

This can be a challenge when the CAE is (as he or she should) working with a dynamic, continuously updated audit plan.

The solution is to work with the Audit Committee and management to not only recognize the need for dynamic planning, but also the need for occasional supplemental budget amounts should new risks and opportunities emerge.

The CAE also should be willing to spend less than the budget!

A Dynamic Audit Plan

> "As I've experienced over more than 40 years in the internal audit profession, change is the only thing that is constant. But I think what is extraordinary now is the pace of that change. It is especially difficult when something new emerges before you have had time to acclimate to and master the previous 'something new.'
>
> "Probably the most tangible effect internal auditors are experiencing from the pace of change is the way annual audit plans are developed and managed. Risks emerge too quickly to rely on one plan for the entire year; internal auditors need to ensure that **audit plans are constantly and consistently reviewed** so they can audit at the speed of risk."
>
> *Richard Chambers in 2021, speaking to KPMG Spain*

---

[17] The picture is from Quotefancy.com. The quote is from C. Northcote Parkinson's "Parkinson's Law", which he included in a 1955 article in the *Economist*: "It is a commonplace observation that work expands so as to fill the time available for its completion."

In late 2006, I had been with Business Objects S.A.[18] as the Vice President of Internal Audit for about six months. I wrote this in my 2007 audit plan[19]:

2007 Priorities and Schedule of Potential Audits

Although it is common practice to develop an annual plan based on an annual assessment of risk, business risk changes constantly. If Internal Audit work is to be aligned with business risks, then the audit plan must be flexible and the assessment of business risk more continuous than an annual event.

Therefore, the plan presented here is an approximation based on today's knowledge of the projects that are likely to be completed in 2007. The schedule will be updated on a regular basis, reflecting either change in business risk or an increased knowledge of risk.

Not every area that represents a risk to the business is an area meriting Internal Audit attention. The only projects planned are those where value is seen in such attention.

Should the schedule of work change significantly, an update will be provided to the Audit Committee.

Based on the risk assessment and an assessment of the potential value of Internal Audit attention, the following projects are likely to be completed in 2007.

---

[18] Since acquired by and merged into SAP, Business Objects was a software company jointly headquartered in France and California.
[19] This is an extract from the Audit Plan included in Appendix III.

	Estimated Hours	
	Non-IT	IT
Available resources[20]	6,250	3,750
Project		
§404[21] testing	2,592	
§404 coordination (APJ[22])	250	
Revenue recognition testing[23] - China	60	
Revenue recognition testing - Japan	80	
Revenue recognition testing - S. Korea	60	
Revenue recognition testing - Australia/New Zealand	60	
Revenue recognition testing - India	60	
Revenue recognition testing - ASEAN[24]	60	
Ethics issue management	150	
Ethics policy and hotline awareness	100	
Sales tax compliance (US)	150	
Acquisition integration - process and measurement	200	
Acquisition due diligence process	200	
Controls over financial forecasting	250	
Americas workforce management	200	

---

[20] Based on 1,250 audit hours per annum per auditor, 10,000 for a team of 8, which allowed for training and other activities. Some use as much as 1,500 hours per person, but we found 1,250 allowed not only for training and time off, but also for the "listening around" I advocate in this book.
[21] §404 refers to the section of the Sarbanes-Oxley Act that requires an annual assessment of management's controls over financial reporting.
[22] Asia-Pacific and Japan, one of the regions (business unit) of the company.
[23] As previously mentioned, the top three financial reporting risks were revenue recognition, revenue recognition, and revenue recognition — followed by corporate taxes.
[24] This refers to the countries in Southeast Asia, a sub-region of the company.

	Estimated Hours	
Privacy/HIPAA[25]		300
Controls over export control compliance	200	
Controls over FCPA[26] compliance	120	
Controls over discount approvals[27]	300	
Sales contract management	200	
Revenue recognition policy awareness & clarity	300	
Controls over duplicate registration of products		300
Information security foundation review[28]		300
Application change management		250
Procurement of professional services[29]	200	
Pre-implementation reviews		350
Restricted access and segregation of duties		200
Director and officer expenses	120	
Continuous auditing development project[30]	250	250
Assistance with investigations	150	
Cumulative hours	6,312	3,778

---

[25] HIPAA refers to the US's Health Insurance Portability and Accountability Act of 1996. This was an audit of controls that assured compliance and protection of confidential information.
[26] The US Foreign Corrupt Practices Act.
[27] Discounting sales to customers was a significant concern. Later I found a fraud involving unauthorized discounts by a sale executive to further his bonus.
[28] Discussed later.
[29] Rather than audit procurement of all goods and services, we focused on professional services as a source of significant concern.
[30] The program focused on revenue-related issues, primarily fraud schemes such as side letters.

I broke out the specialist time (in this case IT audit) from the generalist financial/operational auditor time to make sure I had sufficient resources for all the planned projects.

As detailed in #6 in the excerpt from the text of the plan below, I proposed a team of 8 auditors (in addition to myself): 5 financial/operational auditors (2 based in France, 1 each in Singapore, California, and Canada) and 3 IT audit specialists (2 in Canada and 1 in California).

The budget was based on these 8 auditors. While I had used external resources to supplement my team at my previous companies, I did not anticipate needing them in 2007. I would be able to complete all the higher priority projects with 8 auditors.

I also had responsibility for project management of the SOX compliance program and a start-up software license compliance program (see #5 below). My budget included one director for each area[31].

My audit plan continued:

Staffing and Budget

The budget has been built on the following assumptions:

1. The primary priority[32] remains the testing of internal controls over financial reporting on behalf of management. Not only is this valuable for management, but EY[33] is able to place reliance on some of our work and reduce their fees as a result.

2. The work performed should be balanced, including work on risks relating to all aspects of internal control.

---

[31] The software license program was a great success and I was able to add two more staff in 2008.
[32] This acknowledged the express priority of the audit committee. However, I made sure that the SOX program work did not prevent my team from performing audits of the more significant business risks.
[33] EY was the primary audit firm.

3. Work related to §404 should be no more than 45% of the total work.

4. Staffing should be sufficient to perform all the high priority projects, but not necessarily any projects that are not high priority – either in terms of risk or the value to the company.

5. In addition to traditional internal audit work, the department will also provide:

    a. Leadership (one person) of the global software license compliance function. This is a new global capability, with the tactical performance of compliance reviews performed locally by staff reporting to the three regional VP's of Finance[34].

    b. §404 project leadership and management services (one person).

6. Where possible, staff should be located close to the business. As a result, staff locations are as follows:

    a. San Jose: IT Audit Director (co-located with the CIO[35]), a financial/operational auditor (primarily for corporate audit work), and the directors for §404 project management and software license compliance

    b. Paris: two financial/operational auditors, responsible for EMEA audits

    c. Vancouver: one financial/operational auditor (leading Americas and corporate auditors) and two IT auditors (co-located with the IT function)

---

[34] The corporate Finance function was in San Jose, California, but the Finance functions for the three regions were in Vancouver, Canada; Paris, France; and Singapore.

[35] While the CIO was in San Jose, California, IT Operations and the majority of the IT staff were in Vancouver, Canada.

        d. Singapore: one financial/operational auditor, responsible for APJ audits (co-located with APJ management)
    7. It is more effective as well as more efficient (less supervision is required) to build the team with more experienced personnel. They are able to get to root causes faster, identify appropriate business-practical solutions, and communicate effectively with management[36].

The Audit Committee was rightly concerned that I would have sufficient resources not only to assist with the Sarbanes-Oxley (SOX) compliance work, but also to perform the audits that mattered. Note point #4, above.

I was able to inform them that my budget included sufficient resources to perform as many as 28 high-value projects in addition to the SOX work.

But I included the chart below as further information on where the team's resources would be spent.

Internal Audit Balance 2007

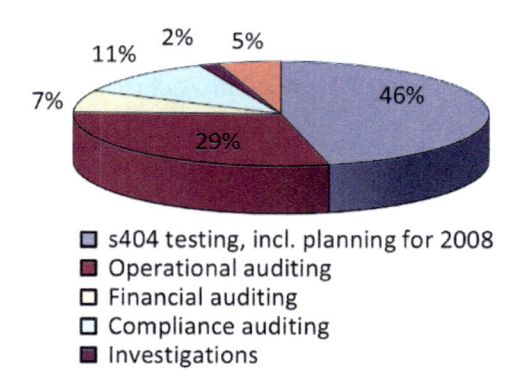

- 46% s404 testing, incl. planning for 2008
- 29% Operational auditing
- 7% Financial auditing
- 11% Compliance auditing
- 2% (unlabeled)
- 5% Investigations

---

[36] I used this approach at each of my companies with great success. The principle is that the time a manager spends supervising and training more junior staff is about the same as they would require to do the audit themselves – with more insight and advice generated from their greater experience.

I will come back to this in more detail later.

When the Budget may not be Sufficient

At a few of the companies where I was CAE, there was tension between the budget guidance from management and the resources I believed were necessary to complete all the high priority projects.

The tension varied from "justify your budget" to "cut your budget!" I heard this last phrase when management, with board approval, saw a need to cut costs because of the economic climate. I was asked, in one case, to sacrifice (which is how it felt) one of my precious team. In another, I was asked to "make a contribution". A third directed me to cut 10%, as every department in the company had been directed[37].

In each case, I talked to the chair of the Audit Committee before the committee meeting. He advised me to listen (but not necessarily obey) management. I was able to persuade the Audit Committee to approve a budget that involved cutting less than management asked. But in one sad situation I had to let a valued person go.

The approach I took was to provide the Audit Committee with the information they needed to set the *right* budget.

Over the years, I developed an ABCD rating system for each potential audit project:

- A. **A *high priority* project based on risk and/or budget.**
  These are must-do audits for one of several reasons:
    - It is required by the regulators. For example, at the oil refining company, there was a

---

[37] This is an awful way to right-size as it ignores how that level of cuts would affect the operation of the company. I tried to point this out to the CFO, who glared at me in response. The across-the-board cuts were made, and people laid off. Several had to be hired back a short time later, although that was done much more quietly. Targeted cuts are far better, where the risk is considered acceptable.

requirement to audit the company's free trade zones[38] every year.

In some heavily regulated industries, the regulators impose requirements on the company to include certain areas in the audit plan. There are some (in my opinion short-sighted) regulators who require the internal audit function to cover the whole organization over a number of years[39]. I have not had that situation but would try to help them understand the risk-based approach; hopefully, they would understand that it is best not only for the company but for the regulators as well. I would point to several laws and regulations, such as the UK Bribery Act of 2010, that require a risk-based approach.

- It was requested by the Audit Committee. I always try to accommodate their requests. The exception is where the request is made by a single director without support from the others and I can persuade him or her that there are higher priority projects.

- The *risk* to enterprise objectives is seen by management as well as internal audit as very high and both believe internal audit can add significant value through either an assurance or consulting project. In some cases, the project was requested by management – but the fact that management requested a project doesn't automatically make it a high priority for internal audit.

    Most of the audit engagements in the plan fall into this category of potentially high risk and value.

---

[38] The federal government required the company to perform audits of the information provided to Customs about merchandise flowing into and out of the free trade zones.
[39] In olden days, this was referred to a cycle-based auditing.

- The *value* of an internal audit project is seen by both internal audit and management as very high. For example, the CEO of the oil refining division believed our presence, performing an audit during a major maintenance project[40], not only had intrinsic assurance and consulting value but deterred contractors from excessive billing. These projects might be suggested by either management or internal audit.

B. **A *'should do'* audit, time permitting**. I would endeavor to perform all these audits but would recognize that the return (to management and the board) on our investment might be lower than those in the top tier. They might relate to high-risk areas where the value of an audit would not be as high. For example, where there is no indication that controls are not sufficient to address the high risk.

C. **A *'may do'* project, time permitting**. These would relate to moderate risk or value projects where the value is clear but lower than in the higher tiers. I would usually try to perform at least some of these audits.

D. **A project where the result would not be of sufficient value**. Even audits of high-risk areas could fall into this category. For example, at one company the utilization of our many factories was typically only 40% (often less). This was not sustainable (and later led to the failure of the company). However, management had a team of excellent people already working on it and any audit would have been superfluous. (The company failed because top management failed to make the hard decisions recommended by the team to close and consolidate operations.)

This results in something like the following. It is based on an actual audit plan I had at Tosco Corporation for our US East Coast Refining

---

[40] The company would spend more than a million dollars each day on work performed by contractors.

Auditing at the Speed of Risk with an Agile, Continuous Audit Plan

operation[41] at a time when the company was experiencing a downturn and the CFO had asked me to cut my budget and staff by 10%.

	AUDIT TITLE	**SCOPE**	**TOTAL**	**FINANCIAL**	**IT**
A	Accounts Payable Controls - Bayway[42]	Review of Accounts Payable controls including approval authorizations.	120	120	0
A	Comets[43] Company Wide Project	Post-implementation review.	120	0	120
A	East Coast Power Construction Contract Joint with Contracts Audit.	Review of all construction contracts.	200	200	0
A	Foreign Trade Zone - Bayway	Review of all procedures, controls, and compliance with all Foreign Trade Zone regulations.	120	120	0

---

[41] Each of my direct reports had their own plan, which I was able to integrate for my higher level review and reporting to the Audit Committee.
[42] Bayway was our major oil refinery in New Jersey.
[43] A major revenue cycle system.

	AUDIT TITLE	SCOPE	TOTAL	FINANCIAL	IT
A	Inventory Accounting Consolidation, Evaluation & Roll-up for East Coast Refineries and Terminals	Review of the entire East Coast Inventory evaluation, roll-up, and gain and loss through the Comets system.	200	120	80
A	Outstanding Findings - East Coast Refining (Jan-00)	All open outstanding findings.	40	40	0
A	Outstanding Findings - East Coast Refining (July-00)	All open outstanding findings.	40	40	0
A	Polypropylene Project[44]	Review of all construction contracts.	200	200	0
A	Assessment of Raw Material Costs (Crude and Cat Feed).	Review of the entire East Coast Raw Material evaluation and rollup through the Comets system.	120	120	0
A	Reformulated Gasoline Bayway[45]	Regulatory audit to ensure compliance with guidelines	800	800	0
A	Reformulated Gasoline Beaumont	Regulatory audit to ensure compliance with guidelines	120	120	0

---

[44] A major construction project
[45] The audits were required by the regulators.

	AUDIT TITLE	SCOPE	TOTAL	FINANCIAL	IT
A	Solid Waste Disposal - Environmental Compliance	Regulatory audit to ensure compliance with guidelines, including a visit to the dump site	120	120	0
A	Enterprise EMPAC Security and Upgrade Plus E-Security	Evaluation of Controls and Security designed into EMPAC, plus any parts of EMPAC not being used and why.	120	0	120
A	Network Security Assessment - Bayway	Continuously run the ISS software for this location and work with the location to fix all high-risk security vulnerabilities found.	100	0	100
A	Novell Security Assessment - Bayway	Continuously run the Kane software for this location and work with the location to fix all high-risk security vulnerabilities found.	100	0	100

	AUDIT TITLE	SCOPE	TOTAL	FINANCIAL	IT
A	Comets Security. This Audit will be coordinated with Phoenix IT Audit	Review of Comets security for the East Coast Locations.	120	0	120
A	IT Change Management	Assess the controls over the approval, testing, and implementation of changes in the Bayway IT environment.	200	0	200
A	IT Access Controls	Review the controls over granting and maintaining access to the Bayway systems.	200	0	200
A	Independent Contractor Guidelines Compliance.	Review Independent Contractor Contracts to assure that they comply with IRS Contractor/ Employee Guidelines.	140	140	0
A	Exchanges	Review of Exchange Accounting at Bayway	200	200	0
B	Catalyst & Chemicals	Review of Procurement and Recovery Procedures.	80	80	0

Auditing at the Speed of Risk with an Agile, Continuous Audit Plan

	AUDIT TITLE	SCOPE	TOTAL	FINANCIAL	IT
B	Procurement of Computer Hardware and Software	Review of Procurement and disposal of excess equipment procedures.	80	0	80
B	IT Disaster Recovery - Bayway	Review of existing IT Disaster Recovery Procedures for Bayway.	120	0	120
B	Bayway Traffic	Review controls for contracting rail and trucking services.	120	120	0
B	Process Safety Management (Coordinate this audit with the Corporate Risk Management Process audit and OPPPA review that will be coordinated with J.H. Corbitt[46].	Review compliance of safety procedures and follow up of near misses.	80	80	0
	TOTAL		3,860	2,620	1,240
C	Accounts Receivable - Bayway	Review controls over granting customer credit	80	80	0
C	Fixed Assets	Review controls over retirement of assets	80	80	0

---

[46] Corbitt was a firm hired by the corporate risk management function.

	AUDIT TITLE	SCOPE	TOTAL	FINANCIAL	IT
C	Human Resources	Assess controls over obtaining background checks for new employees	80	80	0

This time, no A priority projects were sacrificed on the altar of across-the-board cuts. Neither the CFO nor the Audit Committee were prepared to give them up. In addition, several of the B projects were of great interest to both top management and the Audit Committee members, and they wanted them retained.

The Tosco Audit Committee urged me to adhere to management guidance as much as possible. But top management and the Audit Committee were persuaded to allow me to retain sufficient budget to complete all the A and B projects listed above. Sadly, I was forced to let one precious IT auditor go.

Using the same approach several years later, I was able to limit the mandated 10% broad-brush cut at Solectron when the CFO and CEO demanded it, but I had to give a little. I was able to cut co-sourcing and training without losing any of my staff.

This approach made it easy for the Audit Committee and management to see the effects of a budget cut as well as a budget increase. They could then make an informed business decision.

I was lucky in that the Audit Committee gave me sufficient resources at each company to at least address the "A" and "B" projects. However, not everybody is as lucky.

This approach enables the Audit Committee to see the cost of limiting the internal audit budget. We have to trust they will make the right decision for the business.

When resources are limited, it becomes even more important to ensure every dollar in the budget and every hour of internal audit time are maximized. They need to be spent frugally on risks and opportunities that matter to the top of the organization.

A word about the "C" projects and even the "D" projects. Every year, these projects are probably going to be considered again. The more time passes without an audit, the more likely that the CAE will decide that the level of risk justifies moving a "C" project up the priority scale.

While some people believe it is necessary at some point in time to audit every business unit and process, I do not. Every year, I only audit those areas where there is significant risk and/or value. It is highly likely that some areas will never meet those criteria.

Defining the Resources

Once I have determined what I want to accomplish in the period (subject to changes in risks and business conditions), I can turn my attention to how I will perform those activities.

I have options:

- Use only internal audit staff
- Use only external staff – essentially outsourcing the internal audit function
- Use a combination of the two, using co-sourcing to supplement the internal audit staff
- Use one of the above and supplement the internal audit staff by borrowing resources from other functions within the company – "guest" auditors

Over my 20+ years as CAE, I:

- Used co-sourcing regularly to supplement the staff when I needed specialist knowledge. For example, I hired specialists in:
    - commodity trading
    - white hat hacking

- o procurement
- o sales contract management

- Used co-sourcing for audits in nations where my team did not have the local language and that would inhibit performance. When we were going to audit our Solectron operation in Japan, I found out that local management did not speak English. I engaged PwC to perform the audit for me.

- Used guest auditors not just to supplement the level of resources but also to add experience and insight. At Solectron, this was very useful for assessing manufacturing-related processes.

- Hired specialists onto the team when it was clear I needed that expertise on a recurring basis. At Tosco, I hired a certified environmental compliance auditor and an engineer.

- Generally hired a high ratio (compared to others) of IT auditors, preferring those who made sure they understood the business and audited within that context. At Tosco, 25% of my audit team were IT auditors. This reflected the fact that each company was highly dependent on technology.

The key is to define the *type* of resources you need for each project, which I have shown in the examples above.

In my earlier books, especially *Auditing that Matters* and *World-Class Internal Auditing*, I talked about my approach to internal staffing. I like to hire only experienced staff, usually at the manager level, as that:

- Improves the competence of the team and the insights and value they can deliver
- Enables the audits to be completed faster
- Helps the team focus on what matters and eliminate what does not from the scope of work
- Turns out to be less expensive than hiring more junior staff and the managers whose time is spent supervising, training,

reviewing, and generally managing the rest of the team. Instead of my best and most experienced auditors using their time for administration, they were assessing business risks and controls

Some companies have a management training program that has fast-track employees spend time as a member of the audit team. While they may not have auditing and interviewing skills, they bring with them deep insight into the business that can be of great value. At Dow Chemical, Doug Anderson was the CAE and he tells me that "80% of my staff were rotational to/from other departments in the company. In combination with experienced externals hires, they can bring real value to internal audit".

Larry Harrington had an interesting approach to hiring at Raytheon. He says: "we created a mission for Raytheon Internal Audit Create Positive Change with a Sense of Urgency. We only hired people we thought truly understood the mission and reinforced it every day with team members and customers. IA functions need to focus on brand and image too, as a way to build trust, be invited to the table, and sought out to help".

This is somewhat similar to my approach, which was to hire people for their imagination and creativity, their business rather than audit mentality, and their desire to help the organization succeed. Auditing skills are easier to learn than the right mindset.

Sometimes, specialized training for the team is required and should be included in the staff training plan. For example, Tosco decided to use derivatives, both exchange-traded futures contracts and "swaps[47]" with other companies, to hedge its purchases of crude oil

---

[47] *Investopedia* tells us that "A commodity swap is a type of derivative contract where two parties agree to exchange cash flows dependent on the price of an underlying commodity. A commodity swap is usually used to hedge against price swings in the market for a commodity, such as oil and livestock. Commodity swaps allow for the producers of a commodity and consumers to lock in a set price for a given commodity. Commodity swaps are not traded on exchanges. Rather, they are customized deals that are

and its sales of refined products. The Audit Committee mandated that I had to take training in derivatives and make this area a high priority for my team. As mentioned earlier, at first I used co-sourcing to lead the derivative trading audits while I participated as a staff member and learned. In time, I hired an auditor with trading experience.

Another matter that needs to be considered at this time is whether tools like analytics would add value to, or even be necessary for the projects. Some of the projects included in the last audit plan, above, included the use of specialized tools to assess information security.

If any purchases or subscriptions to software or other services are needed by the projects in the plan, then the necessary funds are included in the budget.

---

executed outside of formal exchanges and without the oversight of an exchange regulator.

4. IT Audit Planning

"There is no such thing as IT risk, only business risk." Jay Taylor, former head of IT Audit at GM

This will be a short chapter, as its message is this:

There is no *separate* IT audit plan. It is fully integrated with the internal audit plan.

There is no *separate* IT audit risk assessment. It is an integral element in the internal audit risk assessment and planning process.

Each of the audit plans I have included in the previous chapter had both financial/operational and IT audit projects.

As I noted in that chapter, it is important to distinguish the specialist hours required so that resource planning can be performed.

This applies whether we are talking about IT audit specialists or other resources, such as environmental compliance or safety audit specialists.

In Chapter 5 on Risk Assessment, I will explain how to identify the *IT-related sources of risk that matter to the achievement of enterprise objectives* given the context of other business controls. That exercise is a continuation of internal audit's *business* risk assessment activity, and it will help determine what in the technology space merits an audit.

5. Risk Assessment

"Is our internal audit plan risk-based and flexible and does it adjust to changing business and risk conditions?" KPMG, 'On the Audit Committee Agenda', 2021

As noted in chapter 2, IIA Standards call for a "risk-based plan".

But what is a "risk-based plan"?

Let's first look at IIA guidance.

IIA Guidance
Standard 2010

The Standards don't help. In fact, they point practitioners in the wrong direction! While *Standard 2010 – Planning* is fine, it doesn't go far enough. It says (to repeat it from Chapter 2):

> **2010 – Planning**
>
> The chief audit executive must establish a risk-based plan to determine the priorities of the internal audit activity, consistent with the organization's goals.
>
> **Interpretation:**
>
> *To develop the risk-based plan, the chief audit executive consults with senior management and the board and obtains an understanding of the organization's strategies, key business objectives, associated risks, and risk management processes. The chief audit executive must review and adjust the plan, as necessary, in response to changes in the organization's business, risks, operations, programs, systems, and controls.*
>
>> **2010.A1** – The internal audit activity's plan of engagements must be based on a documented risk assessment, undertaken at least annually. The input of senior management and the board must be considered in this process.

> **2010.A2** – The chief audit executive must identify and consider the expectations of senior management, the board, and other stakeholders for internal audit opinions and other conclusions.
>
> **2010.C1** – The chief audit executive should consider accepting proposed consulting engagements based on the engagement's potential to improve management of risks, add value, and improve the organization's operations. Accepted engagements must be included in the plan.

This Standard explains, correctly, that the CAE needs to obtain an understanding of the organization's strategies, key business objectives, associated risks, and risk management processes.

In other words, we are talking about risks to the *organization's* strategies and objectives. This interpretation is consistent with *Standard 2120 – Risk Management*, which requires the auditor (in the Interpretation) to assess whether:

- Organizational objectives support and align with the organization's mission.
- Significant risks [to those objectives] are identified and assessed.

Standard 2010 continues by requiring the CAE to understand how the organization manages those risks.

The IIA has also issued Implementation Guidance[48], which is considered "recommended guidance" by the IIA. It describes practices for effective implementation of The IIA's *Core Principles, Definition of Internal Auditing, Code of Ethics*, and Standards.

It starts with:

> The internal audit plan is intended to ensure that internal audit coverage adequately examines areas with the greatest

---

[48] Published in 2019, a compilation of the Implementation Guides is available on the IIA web site.

exposure to *the key risks that could affect the organization's ability to achieve its objectives*.

The Guide has other useful advice:

- The CAE's preparation usually involves reviewing the results of any risk assessments that management may have performed. The CAE may employ tools such as interviews, surveys, meetings, and workshops to gather additional input about the risks from management at various levels throughout the organization, as well as from the board and other stakeholders.

- This review of the organization's approach to risk management may help the CAE decide how to organize or update the audit universe[49], which consists of all risk areas that could be subject to audit, resulting in a list of possible audit engagements that could be performed. The audit universe includes projects and initiatives related to the organization's strategic plan, and it may be organized by business units, product or service lines, processes, programs, systems, or controls[50].

- Linking critical risks to specific objectives and business processes helps the CAE organize the audit universe and prioritize the risks. The CAE uses a risk-factor approach to consider both internal and external risks. Internal risks may affect key products and services, personnel, and systems[51]. Relevant risk factors related to internal risks include the degree of change in risk since the area was last audited, the quality of controls, and others[52]. External risks may be related to competition, suppliers, or other industry issues. Relevant

---

[49] I prefer to use the term 'risk universe'. Traditionally, the term 'audit universe' has been used to identify the organization's business units, locations, and processes that may be audited. These are two very different lists.

[50] In other words, it is a list of business units and processes, etc. rather a list of enterprise risks and where they should be audited.

[51] It is better to talk about how risks may affect objectives.

[52] While these may affect the level of risk, we should be concerned with the likelihood of a significant effect on the achievement of enterprise objectives.

risk factors for external risks may include pending regulatory or legal changes and other political and economic factors.

The only problem I have, which I will discuss later, is the concept of an "audit universe".

Standard 2201 and 2210

Where the Standards go wrong (in my opinion) is in *Standard 2201 – Planning Considerations* and *2210 – Engagement Objectives*. I have *highlighted* the sections of concern.

2201 – Planning Considerations

In planning the engagement, internal auditors must consider:

- The strategies and objectives *of the activity* being reviewed and the means by which the activity controls its performance.

- *The significant risks to the activity's objectives*, resources, and operations and the means by which the potential impact of risk is kept to an acceptable level.

- The adequacy and effectiveness of the activity's governance, risk management, and control processes compared to a relevant framework or model.

- The opportunities for making significant improvements to the activity's governance, risk management, and control processes.

2210 – Engagement Objectives

Objectives must be established for each engagement.

2210.A1 – Internal auditors must conduct a preliminary assessment of *the risks relevant to the activity* under review. Engagement objectives must reflect the results of this assessment.

While 2010 talks about risks to the *organization's* strategies and objectives, 2201 and 2210 are talking about risks to an *activity* within the organization.

The Implementation Guide for Standard 2200 makes this clear (with my highlights):

> To implement Standard 2201, it is important for internal auditors to identify, understand, and document the mission, strategic objectives, goals, key performance indicators, risks, and controls *of the area or process to be audited*.

This harks back to older methods, where elements of the organization (business units, systems, departments, etc.) were risk-ranked based on a number of attributes, such as revenue size, complexity, prior audit findings, time since last audit, staff turnover, and so on. Those that were at the top of the prioritized list were selected for an audit. A second risk assessment was performed of *risks to the activity*.

In other words, Standards 2201 and 2210 lead the CAE to design audits to address risks to *a part of the enterprise* instead of *risks to the enterprise as a whole*[53]. Instead of auditing the risks to an *activity* in an audit of that activity, we should be auditing the risks to the *enterprise* that arise and are addressed by controls performed at the activity. I have provided examples of that later.

The traditional approach exemplified in 2210 can easily result in:

- The inclusion in the scope of an audit areas that do not represent a risk of significance to the *enterprise*, and
- The failure to include in the scope areas that could be of significance to the enterprise.

I inherited a program designed this way at Solectron Corporation, where I had a team of about fifteen, split between the US and

---

[53] In fairness, several people (including some of my review panel) disagree with my literal interpretation of 2210. They believe that it should be read as asking that the risks at the activity be identified that are significant to the enterprise. That is the approach I advocate in this book, but I do not believe 2210 says that – and I continue to see CAEs perform audits of risks that may matter at the activity but not at the enterprise level.

Singapore. Every year, the audit plan included audits of the larger sites[54]. The scope of each audit was extensive and either the entire US or the entire Singapore team was sent to staff the audit.

The audits included in their scope accounts payable and physical security, which might have been important to the site. (I believe they were there on general principles.) However, issues like sales contracting and the quality of manufacturing were not in the scope of work. These were both identified as sources of significant risk when a broader look at enterprise risk was performed after I took over.

I discovered that the same issues were found at almost every site in areas such as Information Security. In fact, they were found so often that my US-based IT auditor started writing up related findings even before he had started work!

While the local issues were discussed and actions implemented locally, the corporate-wide perspective was overlooked.

When I became CAE and focused more on risks to the enterprise rather than each site, I added audits of these areas to the audit plan:

- Corporate Information Security, especially their risk assessment activity and corporate information security policies. We found that there was no sharing of tools and methods among the sites, let alone information and other resources. There was zero corporate leadership.

- Sales contract management. The various sites separately negotiated contracts with our major customers, even though they were (in most cases) customers of multiple sites. We were negotiating as trees, not as the forest – which was clearly sub-optimal. In at least one situation, two sites (Suzhou and Guadalajara) competed against each other, and only each other, for the same contract. They managed to drive the value of the contract down to the extent that it was barely profitable.

---

[54] These were manufacturing and assembly plants in Penang, Malaysia; Suzhou, China; Milpitas, California; Austin, Texas; Charlotte, North Carolina; Guadalajara, Mexico; Bordeaux, France; Singapore; and Shenzhen, China.

I also made sure that every audit only focused on issues significant to the company as a whole. Accounts Payable at our larger sites was generally well controlled, and there was no need to audit it every year. However, procurement of the materials and components used in our sites around the globe was a source of risk both locally and to the enterprise. I will discuss my approach to that issue later.

IIA UK Guidance

Before leaving the topic of IIA Guidance, we should look at a Position Statement issued by The Chartered Institute of Internal Auditors (the UK affiliate of the IIA). Published in 2003 with the title of "Risk Based Internal Auditing", it captures the essence of the topic:

> The objective of RBIA is to provide independent assurance to the board that:
>
> - The risk management processes which management has put in place within the organisation (covering all risk management processes at corporate, divisional, business unit, business process level, etc.) are operating as intended.
>
> - These risk management processes are of sound design.
>
> - The responses which management has made to risks which they wish to treat are both adequate and effective in reducing those risks to a level acceptable to the board.
>
> - And a sound framework of controls is in place to sufficiently mitigate those risks which management wishes to treat.
>
> RBIA starts with the business objectives and then focuses on those risks that have been identified by management that may hinder their achievement. The role of internal audit is to assess the extent to which a robust risk management approach is adopted and applied, as planned, by management across the organisation to reduce risks to a level that is acceptable to the board (the risk appetite).

The UK guidance is not only consistent with the IIA Standard 2010, but more succinct and clearer. My only disagreement is why the idea that risk must always be reduced or managed. Sometimes, it should be taken or even increased.

Auditing what matters

Auditing that Matters was the title of my seminal book on internal auditing.

The overriding principle was that if internal audit is to merit that coveted seat at the table and be respected for its contribution to the organization and not just a cost center, it must do work that matters to the leaders of the organization in top management and on the board.

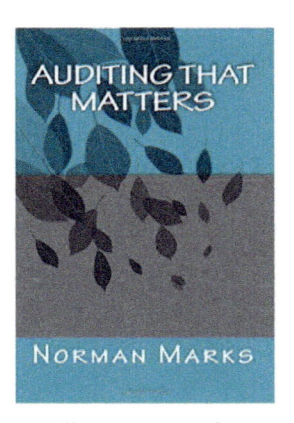

If our work only provides assurance on what happens at an *activity* within the organization, it will matter to the managers of that activity but not necessarily to top management or the board.

> "Almost all of IA findings are mundane operational compliance issues"
>
> - Drew Stein, Professional Chair and Director, and former CEO

In order to do *work that matters* to the leaders of the organization, you need to focus the plan on *topics that matter* to those leaders: the topics they focus their time on and especially the more significant sources of risk and opportunity.

With that in mind, I coined the term "enterprise risk-based auditing".

Using the term "enterprise risk-based auditing" makes it clear that we are interested in addressing the risks to the strategies and objectives of the whole organization.

It starts with enterprise objectives

As the UK guidance states:

> The key starting point is to determine that appropriate objectives have been set by the organisation.

It is debatable whether internal audit should attempt to second-guess the board (who either set or approved the objectives proposed by management).

However, I can see the value in an audit of the *processes* used by management and the board in setting the objectives and the strategies for achieving them. Is the information used in objective-setting, complete, accurate, and current? Are the right people involved? I would include such an audit in the audit plan if I believed there were indications of a significant risk that they were sub-optimal.

But the audit would be on the processes used to set the objectives and strategies; I would not want to provide an opinion on whether the enterprise objectives and strategies were the right ones.

As CAE, I accepted the enterprise objectives as given and moved on from there.

It is not always as simple as it sounds to identify the enterprise objectives and strategies!

They are not always in a list that is readily available to the CAE.

However, one good place to start is with the goals or targets used to measure the performance of top management and set their compensation, especially bonuses.

To this there needs to be added objectives that are unstated, but which would affect performance and compensation. For example, significant non-compliance with laws and regulations, or serious damage to the reputation of the organization, can affect performance assessments as well as bonuses.

I would develop my list with the assistance of top management and review it with the chair of the Audit Committee for confirmation.

Reliance on management's risk assessment

The UK guidance continues with:

> …determine whether or not the business has an adequate process in place for identifying, assessing and managing the risks that impact on the achievement of these objectives.

In other words, how effective is risk management.

That is the topic of another book or two of mine, notably *Risk Management for Success*. I will not dive into the detail covered in that book, except to say that:

> *effective risk management is far more than the periodic review of a list of significant risks. It about enabling the informed and intelligent decisions required to achieve objectives and success.*

If there are indications that risk management is not sufficiently effective, I would certainly consider it as a high priority project in the audit plan. I would use the maturity model in *Risk Management for Success* to help assess and then report on whether the processes in place meet the needs of the organization.

What we are concerned with for audit planning is whether we can rely on management's identification and assessment of the more significant risks to enterprise objectives.

Before internal audit can rely on management's assessment, it has to audit their processes.

IIA Standard *2120 – Risk Management* says:

> The internal audit activity must evaluate the effectiveness and contribute to the improvement of risk management processes.

While I whole-heartedly agree that internal audit needs to do this, it is not necessary every year. If an audit was performed last year and found effective, and there is no indication that it has deteriorated since, I would not rate the possibility of an ineffective risk management program as a significant risk – and so would not include it in this year's plan.

Both the UK guidance and the IIA Standards say that internal controls must be deemed to adequately address the more significant risks before risk management can be seen as effective. Standard 2120's Interpretation says (with my **highlights**):

> Determining whether risk management processes are effective is a judgment resulting from the internal auditor's assessment that:
>
> - Organizational objectives support and align with the organization's mission.
>
> - Significant risks are identified and assessed.
>
> - **Appropriate risk responses are selected that align risks with the organization's risk appetite.** [Controls are risk responses.]
>
> - Relevant risk information is captured and communicated in a timely manner across the organization, enabling staff, management, and the board to carry out their responsibilities.

If t aspect of "Significant risks are identified and assessed" is effective, even if the rest is not, we can leverage management's risk assessment as a basis for our audit plan.

In other words, it is quite possible for internal audit to assess risk management as less than effective as a whole but still leverage it for a list of what management considers the more significant risks to objectives.

Management's list of significant risks is a good start. However, we should not take it as gospel. We should add to it where we believe management may have overlooked or understated a source of risk. For example, management may have assumed that underlying controls are effective while we have doubts.

In *Auditing that Matters*, I talked about an approach taken by Andrew MacLeod, CAE at Brisbane City Council. While I did not have the benefit of a management risk assessment at my companies (until Business Objects), I considered many of the same factors in my internal audit assessment processes.

Auditing at the Speed of Risk with an Agile, Continuous Audit Plan

He starts with the level of (current) risk defined in the enterprise risk assessment. But then he considers the likelihood that the **controls** relied upon to manage risk at that level might fail.

Sources and indicators of **control risk** might include:

- A history of control failures, especially those detected in prior audits
- Inexperienced process and control owners
- Changes to systems
- Concerns about management and their supervision of the work performed
- Changes to the business, especially if there is high volatility
- ...and so on

Andrew would also consider other factors in his assessment of the likelihood that controls might fail. An example would be the time since the last audit of related controls.

The table below illustrates my interpretation of the Brisbane City Council approach.

	Inherent Risk	Residual Risk	Effect of Controls	Confidence in Controls	Adjusted Effect of Controls	Adjusted Residual Risk
	a	b	c=a-b	d	e=c*d	f=a-g
Customer Credit	300	50	250	90%	225	75
Inventory Valuation	200	50	150	80%	120	80
Investments	150	50	100	70%	70	80

The first column shows the level of inherent risk (the potential harm should the internal controls fail). Customer Credit rates highest of the three in the example, followed by Inventory Valuation and Investments.

The second column shows the level of residual risk (the potential harm given the proper operation of internal controls), with the third column representing the effect of the controls. For example, inherent risk for Customer Credit is assessed as 300, but if the controls over Customer Credit are working as they should the level of risk (i.e., residual risk) is reduced to 50.

Taking multiple factors (such as discussed above) into account, internal audit determines how confident they are that the controls are in fact operating effectively as desired. (This is not as quantitative as it looks. The 90% confidence level for Customer Credit is very much a matter of judgment and experience.)

Based on that, internal audit calculates an adjusted value for controls and, accordingly, for residual risk.

For Customer Credit, the 90% confidence level (or 10% lack of confidence) reduces the effect of controls from 250 to 225. Audit's adjusted residual risk changes from 50 to 75.

Looking at all three areas of risk, this model has changed the risk priority. Customer Credit has moved from first to third.

This is one way to leverage management's risk assessment. The main point is that we should use our separate, independent and objective judgment to come up with our risk assessment for planning purposes.

When there is no management risk assessment, audit it

I have presented at several conferences on the topic of auditing risk management.

I was surprised when people told me they were unable to perform an audit of risk management because there was none!

My reply was that the audit can be completed very quickly indeed!

We know what the assessment is: there is no enterprise-wide understanding and appreciation of how one or more risks could affect the organization as a whole.

Now we need to do some work to understand and then communicate how severely this impairs the organization.

It may not be as serious as it appears at first glance. For example, if each activity within the organization is effective in anticipating what might happen and considering that in its decision-making, we have a good start. If that is supplemented through constructive discussion of those significant risks among the department heads, perhaps at an executive committee meeting, then perhaps the big picture of how one or more risks could affect the organization is understood and addressed.

In other words, management may not have a *formal* risk management function but may still be effectively identifying, evaluating, and acting on potential risks and opportunities.

Organizations have been successful throughout history without a formal risk management program or function.

I was asked to establish a risk management program at Business Objects, where I was also the CAE. Our ability to develop new products or enhancements to existing solutions was critical to our success. When I met with the product development team, I found that they were highly skilled in risk management. The managers were all Project Management Institute trained, and that certification has a solid risk management syllabus. They didn't manage from a narrow, project focus, but from a wider business perspective. I didn't want to change anything, other than to integrate what they were doing into my enterprise risk reporting.

One of the benefits of a risk management activity is that it can help the management team see the "big picture". At Business Objects (before it was acquired by SAP and integrated into the larger company's risk management process), each of the direct reports to the CEO identified the same possibility as the greatest risk to the organization.

If one of the mammoth software companies (specifically IBM, Oracle, or SAP) acquired one of Business Objects' competitors in the business analytics space, they could not only propel that company's research and development budget to new heights, but also use their influence with their own enterprise customers to switch away from Business Objects.

All the executives believed such an acquisition was likely, although they disagreed to a moderate degree on how likely.

The effect of just one such acquisition would be very serious. The other giants would look to compete by purchasing another business analytics company, and there would be significant pressure on the board and top management to sell our company while it held a competitive advantage.

Even if we decided to stay independent, our business would suffer.

Each of the executives gave me their assessment of the potential impact. They were all separately monitoring the situation.

But each executive's assessment was different, and the differences were substantial!

I met with the CEO to discuss the situation and his reply was, "they are all wrong!"

Each had assessed the impact from their own perspective, as head of Marketing, Product Development, Finance, Strategy, etc.

Only the CEO saw the big picture.

The CEO put the matter on the agenda of the next executive committee meeting, where they came to a consensus before sharing their view with the board. The board decided to turn the risk into an opportunity, negotiating with both IBM and SAP (using them against each other) to drive a great deal for the investors. Business Objects' competitors were snapped up later.

This is where a risk management function can help, perhaps more than in other areas: bringing views from across the organization together so senior and top management can see the big picture and make the strategic and even tactical decisions necessary for success.

So, if there is no official enterprise-wide risk management program, I would advise the auditor to assess how significant this is to the business.

Does the business have a good view of what might happen so it can make the *informed and intelligent decisions necessary for success*?

If it does, even without a formal program, I would be reluctant to recommend a change that would add more form than substance – and might even impair the entrepreneurship and agility of the business.

When there is a risk management activity

Before we can leverage, let alone rely on management's assessment of risks, we need to determine how reliable it is. As the UK guidance says, we need to:

> …determine whether or not the business has an adequate process in place for identifying, assessing and managing the risks that impact on the achievement of these objectives.

While management's assessment should probably be at least food for thought, the more reliable it is the more useful it will be.

The objective of an audit of risk management is to determine whether the needs of the organization are being met. It should extend beyond compliance with internal policies or conformance to any framework or standard.

The organization needs to be able to anticipate what might happen, both for good and for harm, and be able to address it effectively – so that enterprise objectives can be achieved. Any program needs to be current, updated and actions taken as conditions and risks change.

I am a strong supporter of auditing management's risk management activity, and I recommend using a maturity model such as I have included in *Risk Management for Success*.

If their program is reliable, with an acceptable level of assurance that it has identified the more significant sources of risk and opportunity that would affect the achievement of enterprise objectives, it should be a foundational element in the internal audit plan.

As I said earlier, if management is effectively identifying and assessing risks and opportunities but not effectively "managing" them, we can still use their list. That part of their risk management program may be considered effective even though the program as a whole is not.

Management's assessment of the level of risk for each item in their list is useful but should be viewed with professional skepticism. It will likely be influenced by management's perception of the quality of their controls and, very often, wishful thinking[55].

The auditor's job will be to confirm, or otherwise, management's assessment.

This applies whether management believes the risk is at acceptable levels or not.

As I said, management's assessment is a useful foundational element, but there is more, which I will come back to.

If there is nothing by management, do it yourself

In the absence of a starting point with management's list of the more significant risks, internal audit needs to develop their own.

---

[55] Some good work has been done on cognitive bias. I discuss it in *Risk Management for Success,* but the more authoritative work is Daniel Kahneman's *Thinking, Fast and Slow.*

But be careful: identifying and assessing sources of risk is a *management* responsibility. Being in a position where management relies on an internal audit risk assessment activity, however good it is and however frequently it is conducted, is straying outside internal audit's charter and into management's role.

Management may rely on internal audit to facilitate risk assessment, but they must own it and take responsibility for the assessment.

As the Interpretation to *Standard 2010 – Planning* says:

> To develop the risk-based plan, the chief audit executive consults with senior management and the board and obtains an understanding of the organization's strategies, key business objectives, associated risks, and risk management processes. The chief audit executive must review and adjust the plan, as necessary, in response to changes in the organization's business, risks, operations, programs, systems, and controls.

There are differing thoughts on which come first, strategies or objectives. I prefer to think of management and the board setting objectives for the organization and then deciding how it will achieve them – the strategies for achieving the objectives.

I discussed earlier how difficult it can be to learn what the official objectives and strategies are, and even then there are some unwritten ones, such as compliance with applicable laws and regulations.

So, let's assume that task has been completed and now we need to understand which are the more significant risks to those objectives.

Interviewing the executives

The traditional approach is to interview the executives across the organization and ask them their opinion of the more significant risks.

Very often, they will point to something somebody else is responsible for rather than potential weaknesses and vulnerabilities in their own areas.

If management has not already been thinking about the more significant risks that might affect their operation, and therefore the business as a whole, there is a problem.

This is not only a red flag that management has poor risk management practices, but it is also an opportunity for the internal auditor to help the manager get up to speed. There have been occasions where my team brought in a risk practitioner (or safety or other practitioner) to meet with the manager for a constructive conversation. At other times, my auditor explained the company's risk management policies to the manager and helped them understand why they were important.

A favorite question is:

> What keeps you awake at night?

In my presentations, I joke that the executives never tell the truth when at home: that their young child or other matters in their personal life consume their thoughts and disturbs their sleep.

There are far better questions, such as:

> What do you worry about?

I prefer to ask, in relation to achieving their objectives:

What could go wrong?

and

What needs to go right?

One of the best is:

Where do you spend your time?

I remember asking one of the top executives at Tosco Corporation, Dwight Wiggins, where he spent his time.

He thought about it for a minute or two and took on a surprised look. Then Dwight said that he hadn't really thought about it, but he spent a great deal of every day fighting fires.

We spent the next half hour or so talking about which fires they were, especially whether they were clustered in a particular area. Were there recurring hotspots?

I had a tool that helped many executives focus. I needed it because most of them hadn't really thought through what could happen that might affect their success or that of the organization.

The tool was a diagram (an example from Maxtor Corporation[56] is on the next page) that included many if not most of the areas where there could be risks to the organization.

It was NOT an attempt to consider *all* the areas and rate all the potential risks. Instead, it was a tool to stimulate their thinking.

I also tried other methods such as a mind map[57] (see the second example below from Tosco Corporation) but found the first diagram worked better for most executives and board members.

Everybody is free to adopt it, customizing it for their organization. (I changed it as I moved from an oil refining company to a contract manufacturing business, to a hard drive supplier, and finally to a software company.)

The idea was to help them look at the company as a whole, whether in their mind's eye or through a diagram, and consider the risks to the larger organization rather than only their part of it.

---

[56] A global manufacturer and supplier of hard drives.

[57] Described by Wikipedia: "A mind map is a diagram used to visually organize information. A mind map is hierarchical and shows relationships among pieces of the whole. It is often created around a single concept, drawn as an image in the center of a blank page, to which associated representations of ideas such as images, words and parts of words are added. Major ideas are connected directly to the central concept, and other ideas branch out from those major ideas."

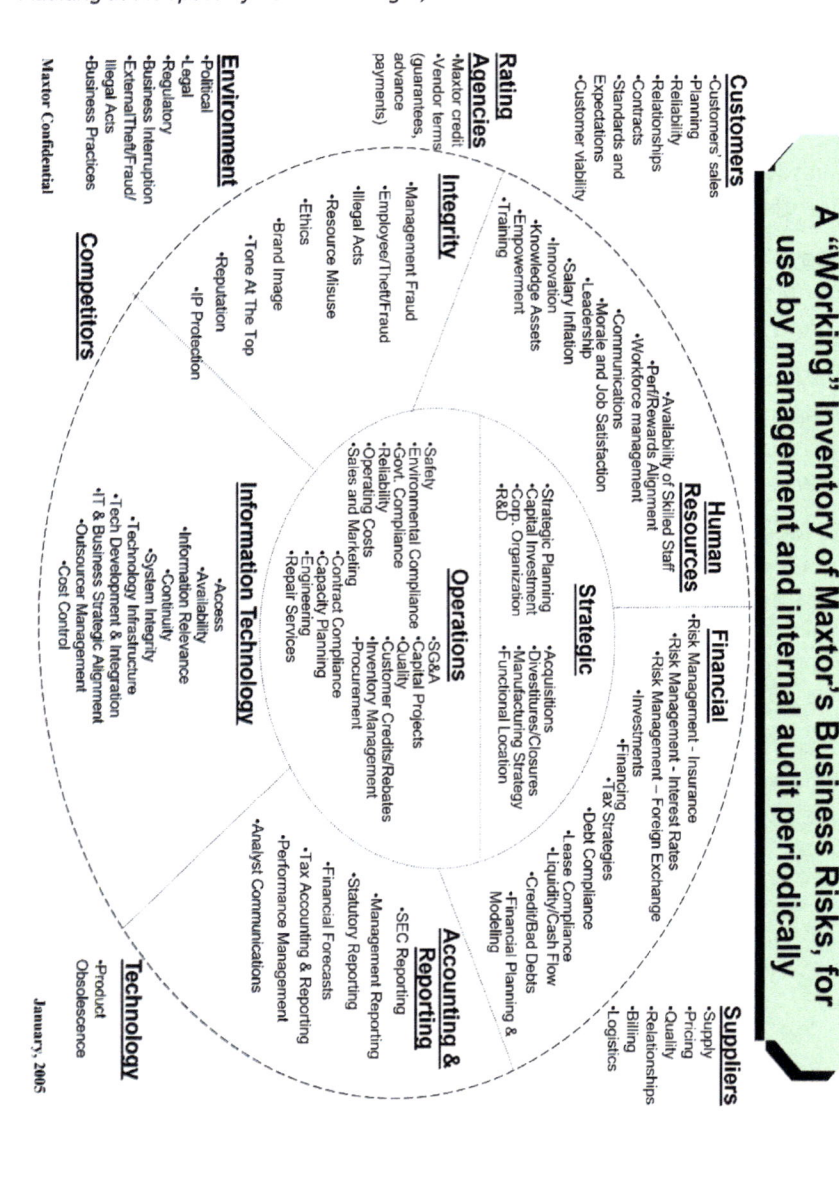

Auditing at the Speed of Risk with an Agile, Continuous Audit Plan

A "Working" Inventory of Maxtor's Business Risks, for use by management and internal audit periodically

Customers
- Customers' sales
- Planning
- Reliability
- Relationships
- Contracts
- Standards and Expectations
- Customer viability

Rating Agencies
- Maxtor credit
- Vendor terms (guarantees, advance payments)

Environment
- Political
- Legal
- Regulatory
- Business Interruption
- External Theft/Fraud
- Illegal Acts
- Business Practices

Integrity
- Management Fraud
- Employee Theft/Fraud
- Illegal Acts
- Resource Misuse
- Ethics
- Brand Image
- Tone At The Top
- Reputation
- IP Protection

Human Resources
- Availability of Skilled Staff
- Perf/Rewards Alignment
- Workforce management
- Communications
- Morale and Job Satisfaction
- Leadership
- Salary Inflation
- Innovation
- Knowledge Assets
- Empowerment
- Training

Operations
- Safety
- Environmental Compliance
- Govt. Compliance
- Reliability
- Operating Costs
- Sales and Marketing
- SG&A
- Capital Projects
- Quality
- Customer Credits/Rebates
- Inventory Management
- Procurement
- Contract Compliance
- Capacity Planning
- Engineering
- Repair Services

Strategic
- Strategic Planning
- Capital Investment
- Corp. Organization
- R&D
- Acquisitions
- Divestitures/Closures
- Manufacturing Strategy
- Functional Location

Financial
- Risk Management – Insurance
- Risk Management – Interest Rates
- Risk Management – Foreign Exchange
- Investments
- Financing
- Tax Strategies
- Debt Compliance
- Lease Compliance
- Liquidity/Cash Flow
- Credit/Bad Debts
- Financial Planning & Modeling

Accounting & Reporting
- SEC Reporting
- Management Reporting
- Statutory Reporting
- Financial Forecasts
- Tax Accounting & Reporting
- Performance Management
- Analyst Communications

Information Technology
- Access
- Availability
- Information Relevance
- Continuity
- System Integrity
- Technology Infrastructure
- IT & Business Strategic Alignment
- Outsourcer Management
- Cost Control

Competitors

Technology
- Product Obsolescence

Suppliers
- Supply
- Pricing
- Quality
- Relationships
- Billing
- Logistics

Maxtor Confidential

January, 2005

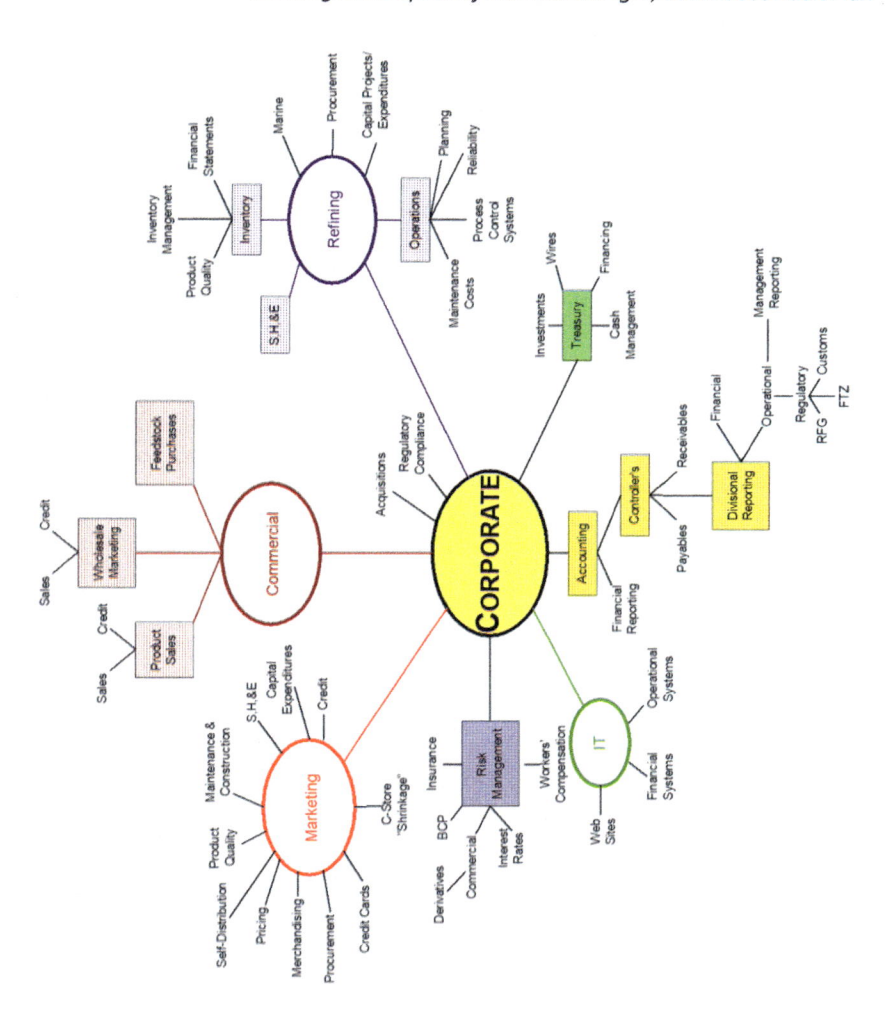

Auditing at the Speed of Risk with an Agile, Continuous Audit Plan

A Mind Map of Tosco's Operations

Getting my interviewees to use one of these as they thought about risks and opportunities broke them out of any siloed thinking. In fact, it turned the meetings into something they enjoyed rather than saw as a chore.

At about the same time that I interview the executives for their individual thoughts, I like to find out what is on the agenda of the executives as a team.

Some organizations are reluctant, but I am usually able to get a copy of the agendas for several months' meeting of the CEO with his or her direct reports. In addition, the CFO (or other top executive to whom the CAE reports administratively) will generally share what the executive team discuss.

It is a fair assumption that the more significant risks are where the top executives focus their time.

At some organizations, a risk workshop can be very effective. This is where a cross-section of the organization comes together, generally facilitated by a risk officer or internal auditor, and they discuss and hopefully agree on what the more significant risks are – and their level.

However, in my experience it is better when the focus is on specific sources of risk rather than when we are trying to identify a broader set of risks to enterprise objectives. For example, I could see an IT audit manager bringing together all the IT managers to discuss privacy, cyber, and other IT-related risks. (If we do that, we should remember that our focus should be on risks to enterprise objectives rather than risks to IT systems or assets.)

In addition to my interviews with the top executives and others, my team members talk to other members of management. I assigned my direct reports and other managers the responsibility of knowing what people like the CIO, head of Compliance, head of Trading, and others are planning and also what they are concerned about. In Chapter 9, I have shared a list of some of the managers we talked to at Tosco.

At this point, I have a fair idea of what the executives think, and it is time to add to that.

Before leaving the topic of interviewing executives, I want to point out that when we move to a *continuous* audit plan, this is something we do throughout the year, not just once for the annual plan. This will be discussed later in Chapter 10, "Maintaining the Audit Plan".

Auditing by Walking Around

So far, I have been talking more about the traditional risk assessment activity.

Relying on discussions with management is not sufficient in my opinion, as they can only share what they believe is happening. But the people in the front-line trenches who are working with customers, vendors, and others every day may tell a different story.

In the same way that management science has the concept of "managing by walking around", internal auditors can keep their ears to the ground by getting out into the field and taking the time to listen to the people in the trenches, as well as management.

I will come back to this later in Chapter 10 on Maintaining the Audit Plan when I address *continuous* risk assessment.

Gathering the views of the internal audit team

It is easy for the CAE to think that that he or she, perhaps with input from their direct reports, knows more about the business and its risks than the rest of the internal audit team.

For years, I would solicit and listen carefully to my direct reports, especially when I was at a larger company and relied on them to build and maintain excellent relationships with the executives in their area.

For example, at Tosco Corporation the company had two divisions: Refining (operating multiple refineries across the USA) and Marketing (with gas stations and convenience stores from coast to coast). Refining had its headquarters in New Jersey, and I had teams there and in California, each led by a Director reporting to me; Marketing's HQ was in Phoenix, Arizona, where I had another team and Director.

While I made sure to have constructive, business-oriented one-on-one meetings with the two CEOs every month, I relied on my direct reports to have a close relationship with the next level down. I needed their input to supplement the information I gathered from the division CEOs.

My three directors not only had a deeper understanding of the business operations, their strategies, challenges, and risks, but also were very good at assessing the strengths and weaknesses of the management teams.

This was invaluable. In fact, the first cut of an audit plan was always developed by the Audit Directors – but we will come to that later.

That worked well, but it could be improved.

One year, I decided to involve the rest of the internal audit team (which was about 50 people by then) in risk assessment and planning. While I left my Directors in California and New Jersey to lead the workshops there, I chaired the one in Phoenix.

I told the Phoenix Director that his job was to listen, because I wanted to hear directly from the staff.

What I heard blew me away. I knew they were experienced, business-oriented individuals, but their insights and ideas were excellent. They raised several points about risks and our ability to help management navigate them that neither the Director nor I had thought of.

Clearly, I should have done this much earlier.

The next stop in my risk assessment journey was with each of the members of my board's Audit Committee.

Discussions with the Audit Committee

While some CAEs may sit down with the chair of the Audit Committee, I prefer to sit down at least once a year (usually several times each year) with each member of the committee for a one-on-one meeting.

I had multiple motives, including:

- Building and maintaining a trusted relationship with each of the directors.

- Helping them gain assurance that internal audit, under my leadership, was working on what matters to them and providing them the information they needed as directors responsible for oversight of management and internal audit.

- Helping them with any questions they might have had about the company and its business. I have found that sometimes they would ask me questions that they were reluctant to ask at the board meeting or of senior management.[58]

- Listening to their views on the organization's challenges, risks, and opportunities – and sharing views where I had different perspectives or wanted further insight. For example, with one director I sensed he had some discomfort with the CFO. I was able to draw him out and confirm that to be true, and later found that the discomfort was broader though my discussions with the other members[59].

I found the first diagram above was very useful when talking to the directors, better than the mind map. In fact, one director found it so useful he persuaded me to talk to the CEO and the rest of the Audit Committee about taking on the role of Chief Risk Officer in addition to that of Chief Audit Executive! But that's another story.

It can also be interesting to discuss the section on Risk Factors (which may go by another name) that is included in the filings with the

---

[58] There were a couple of examples of this. Every new member of the Audit Committee met with me for an orientation session. In addition, some members were afraid of embarrassing themselves by asking questions with the other directors around that demonstrated their ignorance or a poor command of the English language. I was able to help.

[59] This led to an interesting discussion about the CFO with the CEO. The CEO knew about the concern and was addressing it.

© Norman Marks, 2022, all rights reserved

regulators. My experience is that while for some this can be useful, most of the directors see the section (as I do) as "boiler plate". It's a list of risks that includes both significant and highly unlikely events and situations without indicating which they are.

One way or another, whether relying on management's assessment or not, we will have a list of sources of risk to the organization's objectives.

This is not sufficient, yet, to build the audit plan.

We need to consider:

- Where internal audit can add value, and
- What the best audit project should be for each source of risk (and opportunity).

It's not just about the downside of risk

A quick word about *opportunities*, and then we should talk about *value*.

The 'risk' of losing opportunities

Internal audit traditionally focuses on whether management prevents or mitigates harm.

But internal audit can add great value by assessing whether management is taking sufficient advantage of what could go better than anticipated, often referred to as opportunities[60].

---

[60] The COSO ERM Framework recognizes that management has to be able to identify and address the possibility of positive effects from future events and situations as well as the possibility of harmful effects. They refer to these as risks and opportunities. The ISO 31000:2018 global risk management standard includes opportunities within their definition of risk.

Is management overly risk averse? Are they are making poor business decisions because they are unable to see when risks are worth taking, and limiting the success of the organization?

Let's consider some real-life examples.

One of the challenges for any sales executive is deciding how best to deploy his or her sales team. Should the best performing salesperson be given the largest customers, hoping to extract maximum orders? Or should that individual be asked to work with the most challenging customers, hoping to realize revenue that others have been unable to obtain? In fact, who is the best salesperson: the one with the greatest revenue who may have left a lot on the table or have granted significant discounts; or the one who managed to turn a reluctant customer into a highly profitable one?

An audit of this area might identify ways in which the sales personnel could be better deployed for maximum total return (looking at net profit rather than revenue, since discounts can help revenue but hurt the bottom line). Perhaps the auditor can identify how better data mining or training could upgrade performance.

My internal audit team found that the sales personnel were demotivated by the way that their management decided who should get which accounts. Many decided to leave, depriving the company of their experience and the relationships they had established with our customers. Others saw that their bonus targets were easily reached and stopped pressing for additional revenues once they were reached.

Our review stimulated a reconsideration of staffing and compensation strategies by the management team.

In another example, my team performed an audit of the sales process at Business Objects. We found that the sales personnel were reluctant to update the customer relationship system. While they had been directed to record progress on potential customer contracts, they found the system more trouble than it was worth to them. So, they kept their records in personal Excel and other files.

As a result, senior management was deceived when it came to understanding whether and when potential sales contracts would be realized. This impacted the reliability of sales forecasting, which then impacted cash flow forecasting, and any financial projections.

However, the greater issue was that senior management didn't know whether and when they should visit potential customers themselves. The head of Sales or even the CEO could meet with customer management to discuss a deal, and their record of moving sales along was impressive.

The inability to effectively deploy and send in these big guns hurt performance.

In each of these examples (and there are many more I could mentioned), we were looking at the opportunities to maximize or optimize performance rather than to prevent or limit harm.

Executives are interested in achieving objectives, and that requires them to focus on both opportunities and risks – and so should internal audit!

Value-based auditing

If you want to perform audits that matter to the leaders of the organization, you have to pick audits that will deliver value.

The value has to be in their eyes, not just yours!

That value could be in one or more of:

- *Assurance* – that the leaders can rely on their people, systems, and processes to work as intended so that they can achieve enterprise objectives
- *Advice* – that helps management upgrade their systems, processes, and even the people involved

- *Insight* – where internal audit goes beyond what they are willing to put in a formal audit report (for which they usually require evidence) to share their professional insight on operations: their strengths, weaknesses, and opportunities for improvement

I have been a proponent of "risk and value" auditing ever since I became a CAE in 1990.

There are three principles:

1. Only perform an audit that will deliver significant value to our customers in management and on the board.
2. Sometimes an audit of a significant source of risk and how it is addressed by management delivers little value.
3. Sometimes significant value can be provided through an audit of a source of risk that is not significant.

The first principle harks back to the premise that we want to perform audits that matter: audits of something that matters, with results that matter, delivered when they matter.

The other two principles point to when we might decide not to audit something even if it is assessed as a high risk, perhaps in favor of something that is not seen as a significant source of risk.

As an example, at Solectron Corporation we had a very serious problem. We were the second largest company (based on revenue) in the electronics contract manufacturing industry[61]. Our customers, people who had us manufacture and/or assemble their products, were some of the top electronics companies in the world, including IBM, Cisco, Intel, HP, Apple, Nokia, Sony, and a host of others.

Solectron had a reputation for innovation, quality, and a dedication to its customers. It had won two Malcolm Baldridge National Quality

---

[61] The other was a Taiwanese company, Hon Hai Precision Co. Ltd. It was better known as the Foxconn Technology Group and was to acquire Solectron in 2007 (I left in 2004) for $3.6bn – probably more than the company was worth in my opinion.

Auditing at the Speed of Risk with an Agile, Continuous Audit Plan

Awards[62] and multiple awards from its customers. In addition, every manufacturing site was ISO 9000 certified (the international quality standard).

The company had grown significantly through acquisition and had revenues of about $17 billion when I joined as Vice President, Internal Audit in 2001. Prior year revenues were $9.7bn in 1999 and $13bn in 2000. However, net income reflected the low margins common in the industry: $350m (3.6% of revenue) and $497m (3.8%) in 1999 and 2000, and a loss of $124m (0.7%) in 2001.

The increases in revenue came with a burden. The companies that had been acquired were profitable but consisted of a great many small plants. By 2002, Solectron operated more than 100 sites around the world. But when you looked at capacity utilization[63], the numbers were low and too many sites were breaking even at best.

Although the company divested a business or two within a couple of years, that didn't come close to solving the underlying problem.

As CAE, I recognized that this was a major source of risk. I considered an audit that would include in its scope management's capacity planning and management, how it worked with customers to decide which plants would manufacture their products, and how it was addressing the fact that so many sites were barely breaking even. For example, how was management planning to consolidate operations?

My first step was to meet with management; I discovered that they had established a task force to address this precise issue. The leader of that task force confirmed all my concerns but said that they were close to completing software that would give them useful information on capacity and utilization. He explained their plans, their remit from top management, and invited me to attend their meetings.

My decision was straightforward: an independent audit that covered the same ground as the existing task force was unlikely to add much value. Instead, I monitored the activities of the task force[64].

---

[62] In 1991 and 1997
[63] The percentage of available space and equipment capacity that was being used. When it is low, it means that equipment is sitting idle.
[64] Unfortunately, while the task force made strong and constructive recommendations, management was not willing to make the changes. The

There have also been times when the risk did not appear to be significant, but there was great value to our customer in an audit.

In my first year as head of internal audit at Tosco, the chair of the Audit Committee, Hugh Flournoy, asked that I audit the controls over the preservation of water and other rights[65] pertaining to our shale properties in Colorado and neighboring states[66].

That took me by surprise because we had zero revenue from shale oil properties and no plans to produce shale oil. (It would be more than ten years before the price of crude oil would rise to a level that meant that production of oil from shale would be profitable.)

Management thought that this would be a waste of audit time, but Hugh stuck to his guns. He believed that at some point in the future, Tosco's shale properties and related water rights would be of immense value.

The audit found that prompt action had to be taken to preserve the water rights, as those responsible for them had essentially forgotten about them.

Value is in the eyes of the customer, and our #1 customer was very happy with the audit!

A more common situation relates to internal audit's role in fraud risk assessment and investigation. In the great majority of organizations, the risk of fraud is not one of the more significant threats to the success of the organization, but both the board and top management look to internal audit for help.

---

company continued to spiral downwards until it was sold to its closest competitor in 2007 (by which time I had left).

[65] In order to produce oil from shale, a significant amount of water is required, and this is a scarce resource in the western states. Specific actions had to be made to preserve the company's rights to use defined quantities of water in its operations.

[66] Tosco Corporation began life as The Oil Shale Corporation. It changed its name in 1976 when it ceased its efforts to produce oil from shale and focused its efforts on oil refining.

Internal audit certainly has the skills to assist when it comes to potential fraud, and the board generally will support internal audit activities in the area, even though they don't qualify based on risk alone. Internal audit may assist with a fraud risk assessment (a management responsibility in theory if not in practice) and the investigation of potential violations of the company's code of conduct and ethics.

I also recognize the value in addressing the needs and wants of top management.

Several years later, a major systems implementation at Tosco was in trouble. IT and Finance management were pointing fingers at one another, and little progress was being made.

The CFO, Jay Allen, asked that my team (who had been involved as consultants on controls and security) determine (a) who was to blame, and (b) what was needed to move forward. Ordinarily, he would focus on the second part, but the leaders of both factions reported to him and he wanted to understand the situation

My two direct reports (a highly experienced financial/operational auditor who had previously worked as a refinery controller, and an excellent IT auditor who also had many years of experience) were part of my team consulting on the project. I asked them to take on the CFO's task. Each was held in high regard by both IT and Finance management and I knew people would listen to them.

Between them, they found the root causes of the problem. In a highly-charged meeting chaired by Jay with both sets of management, they made it clear where the blame lay – and what needed to get fixed.

It worked and the system was successfully implemented.

The point I am making is that if we are to perform audits that matter, the *results* of our work must matter to our customers. That can either be because we are providing valuable assurance, advice, and insight on a source of significant risk. But it can also be because our work delivers huge value for other reasons.

IT-related sources of risk

While people talk about "IT risk", there is no such thing.

We are concerned about risk to enterprise objectives, so we should be talking about "IT-related sources of *business* risk".

In fact, technology is no longer the domain only of the IT department. Technology is integrated into products like automobiles, advanced manufacturing equipment, refrigerators, and even suitcases[67]!

At Tosco, our refinery operations and pipelines were highly automated, and at Solectron our plants used advanced manufacturing equipment. In neither company did the IT functions manage those technologies.

When Exxon performed a risk assessment in the early 1990's, the risk rated highest was a failure of the blending process at a refinery – another activity heavily reliant on technology. They determined that if the blending of jet fuel failed to operate properly, producing defective fuel that caused a commercial jet to crash into a city, the company (at the time one of the largest in the world) would probably have to seek bankruptcy protection.

So, we should be thinking about:

> *Technology-related* sources of *business* risk.

The related questions we should ask include:

- How do we depend on technology to accomplish our enterprise objectives?
- Where could a failure related to technology directly or indirectly matter to the achievement of enterprise objectives? Where and how could it cause a problem that would be a

---

[67] "The Ovis suitcase, designed as a carry-on, uses self-driving technology and complex algorithms to follow beside its owner, and computer vision technology to maneuver around obstacles." Casper magazine, 2019

significant obstacle to, if not prevent, the achievement of our strategies and objectives?

- Where do we need technology-related initiatives, events, and situations to go right? For example, are there technology development projects that are critical to success?
- Is management staying on top of new or changing technology so they can leverage it for advantage in the business? Many companies do this poorly, running the risk of being left behind as competitors use new technology to leap ahead.

By the way, many of the technology risk standards and methodologies talk about risk to "information assets". But we should be concerned with the effect on the *business* and our *objectives*.

For example, almost every organization has identified cyber (the risk of a breach) as one of its top risks. However, they have made this assessment based on headlines and consultants' publications without an adequate business impact analysis – how it would affect their specific business and the likelihood that a breach would impact their operations so severely that it would be a serious threat to the success of the organization as a whole. Studies have shown[68] that while the press reports and highlights a few massive losses, they are relatively rare.

Every organization needs a careful business impact analysis that includes the insights of not only the technical staff but operating management as well.

If cyber, or more broadly information security, is a significant source of *business* risk, then consideration should be given to including it in the audit plan. That can be done either by itself, in a broader

---

[68] The Ponemon Institute's *2018 Cost of Data Breach Study: Global Overview* (commissioned by IBM) found that the average cost of a breach was $3.86m. Their 2021 study reported the average cost had increased to $4.24m, although the average cost of a ransomware attack was $4.62m and the average in the US was $9.05m. Some organizations had much larger losses and every organization needs to assess its own situation, given its specific facts and circumstances.

information security audit, or in an event more extensive audit of IT General Controls[69].

The lesson here is that each organization needs to understand the risks to its enterprise objectives in its specific environment rather than rely on the latest fad.

Rather than diving into an audit of information security, at my companies (most notably at Solectron, where audits of our various sites had consistently identified issues) I preferred to see whether *management* had completed an adequate information security risk assessment.

There was little point in getting into detailed practices when they were built on a shaky foundation.

Soon after I joined as Vice President, Internal Audit, I was approached by the manager responsible for information security (he was in the corporate IT team) and the head of physical security for the organization. They asked for my support for the purchase and installation of encryption software on every executive's laptop. The concern was that the company's strategies and other confidential information, such as pending contracts with major customers and related emails, were on those devices. The executives (their focus was on those at Corporate rather than in the sites) traveled a great deal and sometimes mislaid those precious devices. The encryption would also strengthen security over communications between the executives.

Management had so far refused to authorize the expenditure. They objected to the cost and to the difficulty they saw in using encryption and decryption every day[70]. My visitors thought that my support

---

[69] As noted earlier, in my opinion and experience information security includes controls over the prevention, detection, and response to a cyber attack. IT General Controls includes both.

[70] They may have been executives in a technology company, but they weren't all masters of the technology they used every day. The security managers were unable to persuade them that the encryption software would be user-friendly, and from what I saw it wasn't.

might influence a change. If necessary, I could take the issue to the Board of Directors.

While this all sounded good and worthy of my support, I asked whether there had been an enterprise-wide information security risk assessment.

They had to admit that they had not performed such an assessment. A recent incident when an executive left his laptop on a plane had led to their deciding that this was necessary.

I explained that without a risk assessment, we could not know whether this was the best use of what were clearly limited funds for information security. I volunteered to help them perform one, and after some resistance and time they took me up on my offer.

That early conversation identified a number of IT-related sources of business risk, even before a risk assessment had been completed:

- Without a risk assessment, the effectiveness of enterprise-wide information security was in doubt. In addition, senior management did not know where additional funds should or should not be spent. (It was later found to be a more serious risk than either manager realized.)

- The corporate information security function (and even the corporate CIO) had little influence over what each of the more than a hundred sites were doing. This was a red flag. Inconsistency probably meant there were significant vulnerabilities.

- The manager responsible for corporate-wide information security reported two levels down from the corporate CIO and had little influence. In addition, this was only a part-time responsibility (he was responsible for the operating system and networking software) where he could afford only about 20% of his time. He had part-time assistance from one of his team.

I saw a significant risk in the competence, knowledge (risk assessment in particular), positioning, and resourcing of information security. My predecessor had only audited information security practices at each site; he had not conducted an audit at the corporate level. That became a priority for me.

The more significant *technology-related* sources of *business risk* should be included as potential areas of focus in the audit plan. (They are *potential* audits because they may have to compete with each other and with non-technology risks for space in the audit plan.)

In my experience the IT function has generally adopted sound methods and practices for change management and security. But when technology is deployed and maintained by other functions, the same level of discipline may not be present.

For example, at Tosco Corporation we owned and operated several refineries across the US. Major technology-related risks included:

- A breach by a hacker of our network and application security that enabled the intruder to change pressure and/or temperature settings on the control system for one or more of our refinery units. This could lead to a fire and explosion, killing several as well as disrupting refinery operations for an extended period.

- An error in the maintenance of the application code of a unit's control systems, or in the control systems of our pipeline operations. Again, that could have serious consequences for the safety of our personnel as well as the reliability of our operations.

- An error in the code or operation of our blending systems. As noted earlier, Exxon in the 1990s identified errors in the blending of jet fuel as their #1 source of risk as it could lead to an airliner crashing into a city.

The related applications and even most of the network were owned and operated by our Engineering and Operations departments in each refinery, rather than the IT department.

Our audits (there were several) found serious issues, including:

- Some of the control systems were maintained by third party vendors, often small companies. Our Engineering department had allowed these companies remote access to the units with inadequate security and no supervision of monitoring. It would not have been hard for a hacker to hijack their access.

- Our white hat hackers (I hired Protiviti to do this for me) were able to penetrate the network and obtain root level access to control systems. (They backed out very quickly!)

Identifying technology-related risks of significance to enterprise *business* objectives doesn't necessarily make them "IT audits" that require a technology specialist. Key is to understand where the controls lie so we can devise the appropriate audit project.

Sometimes, there are sufficient detective controls in the business side to detect a failure of technology. For example, if the code of a report used in the bank reconciliation leads to that report containing errors, the reconciliation process should detect it. That detective control may be sufficient to address the related business risk.

We will take that concept, understanding where the controls lie that management relies on, to determine which audits to include in the audit plan.

Third and Fourth Party Risk

Almost every organization relies on services provided by others. Examples include:

- Data center operations, including services in the cloud and managed cyber security
- Valuations, such as of stock options
- Inspections. For example, at Tosco we used third party inspectors to check the quantity and quality of crude and refined products that we received
- Payroll processing
- Product delivery

If these third parties fail to perform controls and other activities reliably, there may be a significant adverse effect on the organization.

The audit team should understand where and to what extent there is reliance on third parties, then assess the level of risk. If significant, consideration should be given to including the issue in the audit plan.

Fourth parties are a more recent addition to the list of 'what could go wrong'.

Most third-party cloud-based service providers rely on services from Amazon Web Services, Microsoft Azure, and others. In other words, our third parties rely on their own third parties. They are commonly referred to as fourth party service providers.

On December 7th 2021, Reuters reported:

> A major outage disrupted Amazon's cloud services on Tuesday, temporarily knocking out streaming platforms Netflix and Disney+, Robinhood, a wide range of apps and Amazon.com Inc's e-commerce website as consumers shopped ahead of Christmas.
>
> "Many services have already recovered, however we are working towards full recovery across services," Amazon said on its status dashboard.
>
> Amazon's Ring security cameras, mobile banking app Chime and robot vacuum cleaner maker iRobot, that use Amazon Web Services (AWS), reported issues according to their social media pages.
>
> Trading app Robinhood and Walt Disney's streaming service Disney+ and Netflix were also down, according to Downdetector.com.
>
> "Netflix which runs nearly all of its infrastructure on AWS appears to have lost 26% of its traffic," Doug Madory, head of internet analysis at analytics firm Kentik, said.
>
> Amazon said the outage was related to network devices and linked to application programming interface, or API, which is a set of protocols for building and integrating application software.

> Downdetector.com showed more than 24,000 incidents of people reporting issues with Amazon, including Prime Video and other services. The outage tracking website collates status reports from a number of sources, including user-submitted errors on its platform.
>
> Users began reporting issues around 10:40 a.m. ET on Tuesday and the outage might have affected a larger number of users.
>
> Amazon has experienced 27 outages over the past 12 months related to its services, according to web tool reviewing website ToolTester.
>
> In June, websites including Reddit, Amazon, CNN, PayPal, Spotify, Al Jazeera Media Network and the New York Times were hit by a widespread hour-long outage linked to U.S.-based content delivery network provider Fastly Inc., a smaller rival of AWS.

While this is an often-overlooked source of risk, the audit team should be alert to its potential to be significant. It is certainly worth asking management whether they have assessed their fourth-party risk.

Governance and Organizational Culture

When I attended an IIA International Conference in Kuala Lumpur, Malaysia, the first keynote speaker was Lord Smith of Kelvin[71], a highly respected corporate governance authority.

Lord Smith opened his presentation with a startling observation:

> The greatest risk to any organization is a successful CEO.

He also referred to the risk that management will be ineffective when the CEO is a bully.

---

[71] He was a member of the UK's Financial Reporting Council, an independent regulator in the UK and Ireland responsible for regulating auditors, accountants, and actuaries, and setting the UK's Corporate Governance and Stewardship Codes. It was in that capacity that he was responsible for the *Smith Report* on Audit Committees in 2003.

I have worked in organizations where there was an excellent management team with a great culture, and one where there were serious problems with the management team and the culture it fostered across the organization.

When the CEO is a bully or has other serious problems, or the executive team fails to work together, the potential for harm is huge.

However, it takes a brave CAE to report that to the Audit Committee! I can say that I took such a personal risk at the problem company, and it was not received well.

Nevertheless, I agree with the IIA that the effectiveness of organizational governance and the culture it creates needs to be considered when developing the audit plan.

Later, I will talk about how a consulting engagement may be more appropriate in addressing governance issues than a traditional assurance engagement.

The IIA Standards talk about governance:

2110 – Governance

The internal audit activity must assess and make appropriate recommendations to improve the organization's governance processes for:

- Making strategic and operational decisions.
- Overseeing risk management and control.
- Promoting appropriate ethics and values within the organization.
- Ensuring effective organizational performance management and accountability.
- Communicating risk and control information to appropriate areas of the organization.
- Coordinating the activities of, and communicating information among, the board, external and internal auditors, other assurance providers, and management.

The 2017 Standards, excerpted above, use the word "must" far too often. In practice, I suggest that 2110 be read as:

> The internal audit activity must *consider* the level of risk to the organization from ineffective governance and culture; when appropriate it should assess and make appropriate recommendations to improve the organization's governance processes.

Note that a true risk-based approach rarely audits the same issue in consecutive years. So, the language in the IIA Standards that dictates that internal auditors "must" audit governance or anything else is unsound.

Rather than a single audit of corporate governance, I would identify those areas that represent the higher level of risk and *consider* including them in a focused engagement (or series of engagements) in the audit plan.

I believe 'governance' includes more than the areas listed in the IIA standard. I would add at least these:

- Setting and/or approving the longer-term purpose, objectives, and strategies of the organization

- Setting and/or approving the objectives and strategies for the period, including targets for the executives and their compensation

- Obtaining assurance of compliance with applicable laws and regulations

- Oversight of the external auditors, including hiring, terminating, and evaluating their performance

- Oversight of the internal audit function

- The effectiveness of the legal function in providing advice to the board and the management team

- Evaluating the performance and setting the compensation of the executive team

- Hiring and terminating the CEO and other top executives

- Evaluating the performance of the board and making adjustments as necessary
- Communications to the shareholders and other third parties
- Ensuring a desired culture across the organization, considering its many dimensions of:
    - Teamwork
    - Innovation
    - Compliance
    - Risk-taking
    - Customer-focus
    - Community awareness

Over my career as CAE, I had discussions with the audit committee about the organization culture and its difficulties. This was especially necessary when my team uncovered multiple (but fortunately less than material) financial statement frauds. I had to consider and discuss with the audit committee whether these were individual cases or the symptoms of a broader, culture problem.

We also performed focused audits of:

- The reliability of the information provided to the board
- The effectiveness of the legal function
- The measurement of management team performance and compensation
- Employee awareness of the company's ethics policies
- Directors' and officers' expenses

Auditing areas of governance and organizational culture comes with a level of personal risk for the CAE. I always engaged the General Counsel, often performing related audits under client-attorney privilege.

> "At Raytheon, we asked the people we interviewed ten culture questions on every audit and provided a quarterly update to the Audit Committee on culture. Key is to make sure management is sharing all necessary information, people feel empowered, are open to raising their hands with issues, etc."
>
> Larry Harrington

6. The Universe

The traditional internal audit department talks about an "audit universe".

For example, the Institute of Chartered Accountants of Scotland says[72]:

> An internal audit universe comprises several distinct auditable entities which can range from a few to several hundred or perhaps even thousands depending on the scale and complexity of your organisation.
>
> These auditable entities are often constructed according to business unit, product or service line, legal entity, regulatory required audit, processes, programmes, or systems. Alternatively, an auditable entity may simply be constructed according to a key risk or key control. In practice, the internal audit universe is often a combination of all or most of the above.
>
> Put simply, if you think of your organisation as a big cake; how best do you slice that cake to arrive at sensible bite-sized chunks that can be easily and effectively audited? Each chunk is an auditable entity and collectively the chunks are known as the internal audit universe. It's a subjective process.
>
> Once the nature and scope of these auditable entities are determined, internal audit will assess the risk of each auditable entity to assist in producing a risk-based internal audit plan which lists the internal audits to be carried out (this process of assessing the risk will be discussed in a follow-up article).

As previously explained, this two-step risk assessment process (which is consistent with the Standards) can lead to addressing risks to entities in the audit universe rather than risks to the enterprise as a whole.

---

[72] An article by Steve Bruce, CA on icas.com dated April 17, 2018.

Internal audit should be focused on auditing risks to the objectives of the enterprise.

Therefore, the concept of an "audit universe" needs to be put in the rearview mirror and replaced with a *risk* universe, which I define as:

> The risks and opportunities that might have a significant impact on the objectives and strategies of the organization, where an audit project is likely to add value.

It is from the contents of this *risk universe* that audit projects are selected to be included in the audit plan.

I like to build a list of these, prioritized as previously explained as A, B, C, or even D potential audit engagements.

7. Which audits should we perform?

"You have yet to do an audit I wouldn't gladly pay for." Dwight Wiggins, CEO of Tosco Refining Company

Once we have identified and prioritized the risks that matter, as well as our opportunities to add value to the organization, we need to determine which related projects belong in the audit plan.

It is not nearly as simple as selecting a risk (such as the ability to source critical components of required quality at an acceptable price that are delivered when we need them) and making that a single audit.

We need to know more.

We need to narrow our focus further.

We need to know which controls to assess: the ones whose failure to perform properly on a consistent basis could allow the risk to rise beyond acceptable limits.

Focus, Focus, and Agility

When I worked as a vice president, internal audit[73] at a medium-sized financial institution (Home Savings of America), I experienced a "light-bulb" moment.

The president's executive assistant called. She explained that her boss had her go through every audit report and highlight the sections that he should read.

Could I do this for her? Could I highlight the sections of every audit report that he should pay attention to?

Frankly, I didn't question why he wouldn't want to read the entire audit report. I knew that the majority of the content was boilerplate

---

[73] I was one of several vice presidents in the internal audit department. I was not the CAE.

(such as the Background section) and that most of the issues should be addressed by lower levels of management.

So, I complied and diligently used a yellow highlighter to draw his attention to the subject of the audit, the overall opinion, and any serious issues meriting his personal attention.

When I became a CAE, this influenced the content of my team's audit reports. I only included what my customers needed to know, and that rarely included a Background section, scope and objectives, or less significant issues.

But more to the point, I asked myself a different question:

> "If the report discusses work and issues that didn't merit the attention of senior management, why was it included in the scope of the audit?"

I implemented what I called a *"focused, risk and value-based audit approach"*.

Instead of a full-scope audit of a business entity or process, I would only audit those aspects that represented a source of significant risk to the enterprise as a whole and its objectives.

In the audit plans I have shared in this book you will see that few audits are more than 200 hours in length.

That is hard for many auditors to swallow!

But 80% of the risk occurs in less than 20% of an area.

If we want to focus on what matters, that is even less than 20% of the processes, systems, and controls.

These days, the consultants are harping on the word "agile". They talk about agile internal auditing, and I have even seen agile SOX testing!

I believe in agility, if not in the consultants' adaptation of the Agile methodology used in software development to internal auditing.

I believe in being sufficiently agile to respond when new risks emerge, or previously known risks change.

There's no point in knowing that there's a new or changed risk and an audit is needed if you can't respond with speed.

Imagine that the CEO or a board member calls the CAE, telling him or her that a venture is in trouble, and asks if the CAE can send in a team to figure out what is happening.

Imagine that the CAE responds by looking at the schedule, noting that the staff he or she would need are busy, and replying to the CEO that the audit can start in three or four weeks.

That is no way to build credibility and earn a seat at the table.

I keep my audits as short as possible so that I can respond with ***speed***, while keeping my eyers laser-focused on what matters to the organization now and will in the future.

As an example, in the Tosco audit plan I shared earlier one audit was on the procurement of hardware, and in the Business Objects plan I had an audit of the procurement of professional services. Rather than a longer audit of all forms of procurement, my teams laser-focused on where we (and management) saw the greatest risk and opportunity.

Choices in Audit Strategy

There are several ways to design audits to address enterprise risks of significance.

Options include:

- An audit focused solely on *one* source of risk, assessing all the key controls relied on to manage it – including automated controls and even IT general controls.

    This may involve including in scope controls operated by different business units in different parts of the world – all in the same audit. I will share an example of this at Solectron in a moment.

- A variety of the first option is to perform a *series* of audits of controls over the same risk within different business units, each with their own report at the end. There may also be an overall report at the conclusion of the series of audits. We did this at Business Objects so that we could compare and contrast control quality in Asia against that in North America.

- Another variety is to perform separate operational/financial and technology-related audits of the same risk(s), either at different times or at the same time. The trick is to make sure both consider controls addressed by the other. There is a risk of identifying weaknesses in, say IT activities, that are compensated for by operational controls within the business. It is important that the scope of each audit is at least reviewed if not developed by the same people.

- A common approach is to include multiple sources of risk in a single audit of a business unit or process. One issue that this can create, if the CAE is not careful, is a failure to see the "big picture". The audit report may focus on controls at the entity or process level, and the overall management of risk at the enterprise level is not assessed.

- Another option, which has limited application, is to implement a form of continuous auditing or monitoring of a source of risk. This can be effective for issues like fraud, where a point-in-time audit can be a useful project but does not provide the continuous assurance that the organization may need. Internal audit may develop and for a period run the analytics or other tool used in monitoring before turning it over to management as a detective control. I will share an example shortly.

Here are some examples of audits my team performed.

> Solectron operated with slim margins. The ability of the Procurement personnel to source critical materials was crucial

not to only short-term profits but also to longer-term viability!

The company operated more than 100 manufacturing and assembly sites, each with its own Procurement team. The teams reported on a solid line to local management, with a less than clear dotted line to the Executive Vice President for Materials at the corporate level.

I decided that we should focus our attention on the most likely areas to have a significant impact on our ability to achieve enterprise objectives.

I could have selected all the larger sites, but instead took the three largest ones: Penang, Malaysia; Suzhou, China; and Charlotte, North Carolina. Not only were these the largest (there were two others of similar size to Charlotte in the US), but they had a solid reputation and were profitable.

My thought was that by comparing the practices at each, we would not only identify areas for possible improvement, but also best practices that could be shared more widely.

To this set of three, I added the corporate Materials function. Under the direction of the Executive Vice President, they established global contracts for the procurement of materials from major vendors that most of our sites (including the three selected for audit) relied on. The top executive personally monitored compliance with the global contracts using analytics.

I put together a team of three: my two direct reports (one had been a director of manufacturing for one of our larger sites in the US, so had great business experience; the other was an experienced internal auditor who knew Asia operations and the management team very well) and my procurement audit expert.

They performed consecutive audits of the three locations, moving from one to the other with short breaks, and then assessed the corporate function before writing a report with their overall assessment.

> In this way, the team was able to identify common weaknesses and best practices as well as specific issues and opportunities at each location.

This was a series of audits that focused on a single source of risk to enterprise objectives.

> At Business Objects S.A., revenue fraud was an historic issue as well as a current concern. During my tenure as Vice President, Internal Audit, I personally conducted several investigations that found fraud.
>
> A common method used by sales executives was to entice a customer into increasing their order volume. They would offer a large discount that would be justified by the larger order, and promise (often in writing) to give them a credit for the return of excess software licenses in the next quarter.
>
> This practice (involving what was called a 'side letter'):
>
> - Inflated revenue for the quarter, a financial reporting issue.
> - Earned the sales executive an undeserved larger bonus because of the higher revenue number.
> - Hurt our revenue and margins because of the discount.
> - Impacted the culture and behavior of junior sales staff.[74]
>
> Unfortunately, the practice was difficult to stop. Controls depended on the integrity of management – who were frequently the people leading or at least condoning the fraud.
>
> I had my team develop analytics that would detect fluctuations in revenue and margins from quarter to quarter, as well as monitor the incidence of credits given to our customers. I encouraged

---

[74] One of the frauds I investigated involved a side letter that was signed by a junior sales staffer, at the direction of a vice president. The junior did not realize that this was wrong, even though it was a clear violation of our Code of Conduct, because he had been instructed to do it.

management (independent of the sales teams) to take this over and improve on the monitoring.

So, instead of an audit of the controls in place, I had a project in my audit plan to implement revenue fraud monitoring with the intent of helping management upgrade their controls.

The approach was continuous auditing or monitoring, as experience had shown that preventive controls by management were unlikely to be sufficient. The plan was for internal audit to perform independent monitoring for a while, then turn over the software and the responsibility for using it to management as a detective control.

> Earlier, I talked about information security at Solectron. The team had performed multiple audits at the site level, and it was clear that the company needed a corporate level strategy and leadership if we were to make any significant progress.
>
> I decided against a traditional audit of corporate information security. I already knew that the corporate team had little influence over the rest of the organization, was under-resourced, and (to be honest) didn't have a sufficient understanding of information security principles and practices.
>
> I had my team perform what I called an Information Security Foundations audit[75]. It focused on the structure and framework of information security at Solectron, rather than detailed information security tools and practices.
>
> I believed that a strong set of information security defenses and response mechanisms depended on having a strong and reliable foundation.
>
> The general results were known before we started, so the great majority of the time taken by the audit was in working with the corporate management team to agree on the severity of the risk and the actions that should be taken.

---

[75] I also included an Information Security Foundations audit in my 2007 audit plan at Business Objects – which I shared on page 14.

> We continued to include information security in the scope of our audits of individual sites. Those audits helped local management upgrade their activities. But a solution for the company as a whole required a different posture from the top, which we helped drive with our Information Security Foundations audit.

One of the challenges in building the audit plan is the inclusion of technology-related audits.

It is very easy to perform an IT audit that focuses on issues that, when considered together with controls within the business, are less important than the IT auditor (or IT management) believes.

> At Business Objects, we routinely audited IT General Controls[76]. This was an audit that our external auditors relied upon, but we defined the scope based on *our* needs rather than theirs.
>
> We focused on IT's controls over the applications that were relied upon, in conjunction with controls within business processes, to address the more significant risks to the company's business strategies and objectives – not just financial reporting (the concern of the external audit firm). Those applications included non-financial applications such as the analytics used by management to monitor activities in sales and other areas.
>
> We excluded from our scope IT activities, such as change management, over applications where an issue would not be significant. For example, the Human Resources management system was unlikely to fail to the extent that it would seriously impede our achievement of the company's objectives.

---

[76] Some have asserted that cybersecurity is different from information security. I don't hold to that view, nor that IT General Controls does not include the controls that prevent, detect, and respond to a cyber-attack.

The most common approach, as mentioned earlier, is to include multiple risks in the scope of individual audits of a process or business unit.

> At Solectron, we routinely audited each of our larger sites. When I took over as Vice President of Internal Audit, we typically performed two audits at a time, each with about half the audit staff of fifteen. One would be by the team based in the United States of a site in either the Americas or Europe, and the other would be by the team based in Singapore of a site in Asia or Australia.
>
> All the audits would be considered "full scope" audits, covering quite a few sources of risk. This approach followed traditional guidance: select the largest sites and most significant processes, then audit the risks to those sites and processes.
>
> That way, the CAE was able to cover the sites that contributed most not only to revenue and profits, but also to risk to enterprise objectives.
>
> However, he only completed audits of 17 sites and left about 100 sites untouched – especially as the level of resources only allowed the CAE to audit the top five sites each year and a handful of the other sites on something of a rotational basis.
>
> As I explained earlier, Solectron's margins were wafer thin. Any of the 100 sites could potentially have an issue of significance to the whole company, especially if the same problem occurred at multiple sites. Given the reliance by several sites on the same systems, that was quite possible.
>
> The first step in my redesign of the audit process was to limit the work done at the major sites. Rather than a "full scope" audit, I only included in scope areas where a problem at the site would be significant to the achievement of *enterprise* objectives. For example, we no longer audited physical security. We also eliminated the audit of controls that had been assessed as effective in the last year, or where we knew there were issues that management was actively working on.

In other words, we eliminated areas where it was unlikely that we would add value.

That allowed me to shorten the length or staffing of these audits, which in turn allowed me to perform additional audits with the same level of audit resources.

I used another technique (a modified form of Control Self-Assurance) to extend the assurance I provided to leadership, which I will discuss later.

Assurance or Consulting?

Most audits are intended to provide assurance, indicating whether management has adequate controls over the risks included in scope[77].

However, there are times where it is better to perform a consulting engagement rather than a more traditional assurance audit.

The situation that most of the commentators talk about is where management asks internal audit to perform an engagement for them.

While the primary customer of an assurance engagement is the Audit Committee with top management a secondary customer, in a consulting engagement management is the main customer. In many situations, there is no reporting to top management or the board. (The exception is where a serious issue is identified by a consulting engagement, upon which the CAE has an obligation to share that information with the board and top management.)

In this situation, the scope, objectives, and the form of the end-product are agreed-upon by management and internal audit.

Earlier, I talked about the CFO of Tosco, Jay Allen, asking that my team assess why a systems implementation was in trouble; I assigned my top two auditors to partner on that task. They communicated the

---

[77] Best practice is for the audit team to express their opinion on the adequacy of management's controls over the risks in scope, but some continue to focus on whether there are control deficiencies of significance. The framing of an opinion is outside the scope of this book, and I suggest instead *Auditing that Matters*.

results orally to the CFO and involved management. There was no formal, written audit report.

That was an example of a consulting engagement that was requested by management.

However, there are times when the need and value of a consulting engagement is identified by internal audit. What distinguishes these cases from an assurance engagement is that, as in the previous example, the primary customer is management (it may even be operating management). Any report or communication at the end of the engagement is similarly addressed to management and may not be shared with the board.

The best example of this is a pre-implementation controls review. This is where management has a project, most often a new systems implementation, where internal audit can add value by helping them ensure that when the system goes live it will have the appropriate internal controls and security.

My various teams did a lot of this, delivering so much value that at Tosco the head of IT told me he would never have a major systems development project without internal audit consulting on it.

I am a huge believer in the principle, borne of years of experience, that most problems occur as the result of change – whether that be from a change in systems or people.

I am also a huge believer in the principle that it is far better to consult on a change initiative and *prevent* a controls or security issue, than it is to perform an audit after-the-fact.

Fixing something that is broken is harder and more expensive than correcting it at the start. There are several pre-implementation (and a post-implementation) review projects included in the Tosco audit plan I shared on page.

The end product of a pre-implementation review is a report, which may be verbal or written, addressed to management that provides them with assurance that controls and security should be adequate upon implementation. Caveats may be included if, for example, we close out our engagement before the end of the project. For example, when we have confidence in management's testing, we may move on to another audit engagement without getting involved in testing ourselves. (Why keep going when there is more value in spending the time on another source of risk?)

A frequent opinion was:

> "If the system is implemented as designed, with the controls performed as documented, and testing is completed without issue, we believe the controls and security should be adequate."

As I said, the communication at the end of the consulting engagement is to management. But I inform the Audit Committee that we have completed the engagement as part of my regular report to them.

Another example is where the focus is on enterprise risk management. When it is known to be less than mature, you want to encourage progress rather than making those responsible for it look bad. I have advocated using a maturity model[78] to indicate where the program lies. This points out the current status, indicates how it can be improved, and lets management see the value of further progress.

This can be considered a consulting engagement if the primary purpose is to report to management rather than the board.

The same principle applies to audits of elements of corporate governance. The IIA shared a Practice Guide in 2012, *Assessing Organizational Governance in the Private Sector*[79]. It states:

> In the process of setting the scope [of an engagement], the CAE will assess the relative risk of governance processes, evaluate the audit approach — assurance vs. consulting —

---

[78] I have included a maturity model in *Risk Management for Success*.
[79] Available in the Recommended Guidance section of the IIA's website.

and identify the various stakeholder expectations in setting the assessment objectives.

It goes on to say:

> The appropriate role for internal audit and the resource commitment ... will depend largely on the maturity of the organization's governance structures and the organization's size and complexity. The CAE should discuss and reach an agreement with the board on internal audit's role in assessing organizational governance.

The idea is that when the processes are seen as less mature, internal audit may be more effective by encouraging and helping improvement rather than performing a traditional audit with the inevitable assessment that practices are inadequate.

What this means is that the CAE should consider how best to add value to the organization.

Is it by performing an assurance engagement that delivers an opinion on the quality of controls and related processes, or is it by helping management upgrade their activities with a consulting engagement?

This is an important distinction. When I reviewed my audit plan with the Audit Committee, I would make sure they understood the difference and what it would mean to them.

I emphasized that even in a consulting engagement, I would bring to their attention (and that of top management) any issues of significance to the success of the organization.

In all my years of leading internal audit, they never asked me to change the approach, although they were occasionally curious why I would choose one over the other.

Reliance on other Assurance Providers

There are times where it makes sense to rely on the work of others, such as the Quality team in a manufacturing company, or the Quality

Assurance function (QA) in IT[80]. The first performs inspections and other work that internal audit can rely on to address risks relating to the quality of the company's products (once their processes, etc. have been found reliable in an audit of the function). The second tests the functionality and reviews the documentation of new systems.

As with reliance on management's risk assessment activity, internal audit needs to audit the function on which it will rely. It needs to obtain reasonable assurance that the function will perform the work to a satisfactory standard, without undue influence from management.

In such cases, I will make it clear in the text of the audit plan that I am relying on these functions for specific risks.

"Reliance" implies that internal audit will not perform their own audit work, but will place full reliance on the other assurance provider. However, there are options, such as:

- Reviewing the work performed by the assurance provider and only testing a smaller sample of controls or otherwise limiting the extent and nature of internal audit testing. This is very similar to what the external auditor does when "relying" on internal audit testing for SOX compliance.

- Downgrading the level of risk assigned to an area because the other assurance provider has audited it. Doug Anderson did this at Dow Chemical.

- Teaming with the other assurance provider on a joint audit. I did this a couple of times at Solectron where the audit team comprised individuals from (Manufacturing) ISO 9000 Quality and the external audit firm as well as internal audit.

One situation where internal audit relies on another assurance provider, but is rarely mentioned, is the risk that materially inaccurate financial statements are filed with the regulators (the SEC in the US).

---

[80] This is sometimes referred to as "combined assurance".

We rely on the work of the external auditor and any management testing of controls over financial reporting, and I will point that out in the text of the audit plan I review with the Audit Committee.

Over my career, I have relied on:

- Third party, independent inspection companies who measure and report on the volume of crude oil and products in refinery storage tanks
- The organization's physical security department for their inspection of perimeter protections and theft prevention measures inside warehouses and factories
- The external auditor for their financial statement audit
- The IT QA team for their independent testing of new or modified software
- The Environment, Health, and Safety team for their inspection and audit of compliance at our refineries, pipelines, and terminals
- Third party ISO 9000 quality auditors in our manufacturing and assembly plants
- Audits of our third-party service providers (primarily IT services companies) by independent auditors[81]

The approach I like to adopt when auditing these functions for reliance purposes is very similar to the approach taken by the external auditors before relying on internal audit's work[82]. The IIA has its own Practice Guide: *Reliance by Internal Audit on Other Assurance Providers*[83].

---

[81] In the US, these are generally performed in accordance with the AICPA's *Statement on Standards for Attestation Engagements no. 18*, formerly SSAE 16 and before that SAS70. Outside the US, there is an international standard, ISAE 3402, *Assurance Reports on Controls at a Service Organization*.

[82] In the US, the auditors of larger companies follow the PCAOB Standard Auditing Standard 2605, *Consideration of the Internal Audit Function*.

[83] Available on the IIA web site under Standards & Guidance, Recommended Guidance, Practice Guides.

Outsourcing

A variation on the above is to fully or partially outsource a project.

This is different from using a co-source partner to supplement a team, where most of the work is performed and led by one of the internal audit team members.

I am talking about a situation where significant reliance is placed on a third party to perform the audit, which may be an assurance or consulting engagement.

That reliance on a third party could be for a variety of reasons, including:

- Insufficient resources (staffing) to perform the audit
- A lack of necessary technical knowledge, experience, or other capabilities
- Travel and other restrictions

I always preferred to handle every audit with my own team, but there have been occasions when it has been necessary to fully or partially outsource a project.

While as CAE I delegated the performance of the work, I was always accountable for the audit and the quality of its results.

Here are some examples of where I outsourced a project:

- White-hat penetration studies of network security at our Northern California refinery. I used a consulting firm (Anderson, later Protiviti) because they had up-to-date technical knowledge and tools. They defined the scope of work under my supervision, but the report to management was by me.
- Audits of our operations in Japan were staffed by local auditors from PwC, as my team had no Japanese and the local management team very little English. My team defined the scope and audit program, reviewed the workpapers, and wrote the audit report.
- Audits of our fledgling commodities trading desk were performed by a specialist firm with prior trading desk and

audit experience. So that we could retain knowledge and build our own capability, I assisted on the first audit and then had one of my managers assist and then lead subsequent ones. In time, we migrated to fully internally run trading audits.

I did not use this option often, as internal staff generally had a better understanding of the company, its business, and its people – and I wanted to build and then maintain the capability to audit even tough topics internally. (The outsourcing option is also more expensive!)

When I did outsource a project, I retained the ability to review the results with the team. I also wrote the audit report myself.

Other Types of Audit Project

There are other ways to perform either an assurance or consulting engagement, and it is important to consider and plan for these in the development of the audit plan.

Choosing one of the alternatives to a traditional audit may require early planning and coordination with management of the area, and it may also require the acquisition or development of specialized software.

Software Project

In the 2007 Business Objects audit plan I shared on page 32, I included 500 hours (250 each for financial/operational audit staff and for IT audit staff) for the development of continuous auditing software.

In that same audit plan, I also had hours budgeted for running software (from Integrated Software Solutions, or ISS) that monitored the activities of the database administration team. This was because the entire DBA team had left the company and been replaced by contractors. The risk of an inappropriate action by one or more of the DBAs was unacceptable, as the only individual monitoring the work of the team was from the same firm. Therefore, the audit team had worked with IT management to select monitoring software that we ran on their behalf. (Our IT audit manager was technically more proficient than anybody in IT management.)

The Tosco audit plan I shared on page 40 also included running software from ISS, that time to monitor security provisions in the local area network.

Control Self-Assessment

Another technique I used to good effect, notably at Solectron, was control self-assessment, or CSA. As noted earlier, we had over 100 locations around the globe and there was a possibility that an issue at almost any one of them could have serious consequences for the organization as a whole.

My team was only about 15 people, so our ability to address more than a few sites with a traditional audit was very limited. In fact, my predecessor relied on traditional audits and was only able to complete about 17 site audits and 5 process audits each year.

So, we relied on a form of control self-assessment.

Gulf Canada, under the leadership of Bruce McCuaig, is credited with the first use of CSA in 1987[84]. In its initial stages, there were two main ways of performing CSA. Both involved management in the assessment of risks and controls: facilitated workshops where a broad cross-section of management discuss the management of risk and the adequacy of controls[85], and questionnaires where internal audit ask management to self-assess their controls and risks. The IIA set up a CSA Center with a newsletter and annual CSA conferences (in 1995 and 1996) in which I was actively involved. They also established a certification in CSA (CCSA) that has since been discontinued.

My predecessor at Solectron had developed questionnaires that covered the more significant risks at a typical manufacturing or assembly site. They listed the controls that were expected to be

---

[84] Tim Leech was a member of Bruce's team.
[85] I used this technique for the first time while I was with a mid-size financial institution in 1984. We also used it in the next decade at Tosco to help management decide whether to expand operations into Mexico with a sales channel partner of doubtful ethics.

present and asked that management confirm both their existence and effective operation. If the risks were addressed by other controls, management could so indicate.

When an audit of a site was planned, he had the site complete and return the questionnaire. It was used during the audit but more as an information source than anything else. Even though he told me that management's representations on the questionnaire were incorrect 80% of the time, that fact was never included in the audit report and he did not make an issue of it with management.

I saw this as an opportunity.

I upgraded the questionnaire and had my team send it to *every* site, not just those where we planned an on-site audit. Each member of the team was charged with being the liaison with management of several sites. They would:

- Review the completed questionnaires and check for omissions, obvious errors, and inconsistencies. I called this a "desk review".

- Have a conversation with management about those issues, identified deficiencies and corrective actions, and anything else management felt we should know.

- Ask management to send additional documentation, such as examples of policies or evidence of control operation, as needed.

- Assess the possibility, based on that review, that controls at the site were not adequate for one or many risks.

- Recommend whether we should have a short visit to the site to discuss the questionnaire and any issues, a longer on-site audit (in which case, the auditor would define the scope of the work) or rely on management's self-assessment.

The CSA approach allowed the team to address a far larger proportion of the global organization. Where we felt the risk was higher, we performed on-site audits that focused on a select number of risks. Where the risk was lower, we relied on management self-assessment. (Note: as I indicated above, we often asked for supporting documentation to be sent to us before we decided to rely on management's assessment.)

This is a form of "trust and verify[86]".

The other change I made from my predecessor's practice is that where management was, without satisfactory reason, providing us with clearly wrong self-assessments that fact was included in the audit report[87].

In terms of the audit plan, I had no certainty where I would have on-site audits nor what level of work I would perform in each. The audit plan indicated an approximate number of on-site audits and the estimated number of hours required[88]. I also had a line for the work done by the team in sending and reviewing CSAs to each site.

I made sure the Audit Committee understood the approach (which they liked) and that the audit plan was at all times an estimate that I would continuously update.

There are other situations where a survey and a review of the results constituted almost the entire audit engagement. For example, an audit of 'culture' or employee awareness of the ethics policy and expectations might leverage a survey. I would work with the Human Resources function to ensure their routine employee survey had useful questions, and review the results. A survey was also used heavily in the 'Revenue recognition policy awareness & clarity' engagement at Business Objects shown on page 32.

Audits of Third Parties

One source of value is the ability of internal audit to audit third parties, either to increase revenue or to minimize costs[89].

---

[86] A Russian proverb made famous by Ronald Reagan in the 1970s, as he discussed nuclear disarmament with the Soviet Union.
[87] We also talked to management to determine whether there was a deliberate attempt to deceive: a far more serious problem.
[88] A SWAG: scientific, wild-assed guess.
[89] Some do not see this as an internal audit responsibility, and I agree. However there was clear value, and I was able to add specialists to my team

Three sets of engagements my teams performed spring to mind:

1. Audits of contractors and vendors for compliance. We did this extensively at Tosco. Each year, my team of contract audit specialists obtained a 12:1 return on investment (actual monies recovered compared to my costs).

   In the Refining division, we found overcharges and other non-compliance, but over time we migrated to providing consulting advice to the procurement team that helped them negotiate better contracts. Instead of recapturing money, we worked with management to stop it leaving our coffers.

   Management liked our work so much in the Refining division that they asked us to increase headcount on the team even when the company as a whole was working to cut costs. The CEO of that division asked us to wear distinctive clothing and hard hats when we were in the field, as he felt it would discourage vendors from manipulating their charges.

   In the Marketing division, we found overcharges in the millions (especially on purchases of tobacco products for sale in our convenience stores).

   At a meeting of the Marketing division executive team to discuss the prior year's financials and the plan for the upcoming year, the division CFO put up a slide with the prior year results. The contribution by my team was a separate line item! When I asked him why, he said it was because the contract audit recoveries of overcharges "distorted the results for the year". The executives then spent several minutes discussing how much they should include in the budget for the upcoming year for similar cost recoveries.

2. Audits of customers. At Business Objects S.A., I had a specialist team[90] that was able to find situations where our

---

to perform the work. The Audit Committee approved my adding this function as a service to management, especially as it did not adversely affect my internal audit team's ability to address the risks that matter to the enterprise.

[90] The team was separate from internal audit but reported to me as a service to management, with Audit Committee approval.

© Norman Marks, 2022, all rights reserved

customers were using our software excessively, violating the terms of the license. If they purchased a license for, say, 10 people and 20 were actually using it, my team would find out and work with management to have the customer remedy the situation – usually by purchasing the additional licenses. We worked with management to minimize customer dissatisfaction over being caught out, yet still recovered substantially more money (revenue) than our costs.

3. <u>Audits of healthcare providers and insurance companies</u>. This is a fairly common practice for internal auditors, where they determine whether they are being overcharged, for example for employees who have the left the organization. Our audits were able to confirm the charges we received were accurate, but I have heard of other internal audit teams identifying serious problems with the billing.

Since I had specialized teams performing the first two types of audit engagement, I did not include them in the list of audits in the audit plan. Instead, I had sections in the text document that explained what they were doing.

However, I would include healthcare provider audits in the list of audit engagements. I considered them a type of consulting engagement.

Investigations

In each of my companies, the internal audit team (including me) would perform investigations of potential violations of the Code of Conduct[91].

In general, I simply stated that in the text without any line items in the list of audit engagements. However, when I believed they would consume a significant of time, I allowed for it in my resource planning.

---

[91] Some CAEs believe that investigations should not be performed by internal audit but are a management responsibility. This is something that should be discussed and agreed with both management and the Audit Committee. We documented which investigations should be performed by internal audit (such as fraud) and which should not (such as harassment).

Assistance to the External Auditor

The audit plan I shared earlier for Tosco was for just our Bayway refinery operations. However, we also had separate but integrated plans for our other operations. One of those was the Trainer refinery near Philadelphia that we had recently acquired. That audit plan included 180 hours for assisting PwC with their first year financial audit. It was mostly coordination and covered all the major financially relevant systems and procedures.

In general, I prefer to use my team to perform audits focused on the more significant business risks. However, there are times when I put my business hat on and consider what is best for the company as a whole.

If and only if I can complete my preferred audits of the more significant risks, I will dedicate some number of hours to external audit assistance.

In the past, I have been able to hire contractors, not for that specific assignment, but to backfill the hours for which I am essentially lending staff to the external audit firm.

But it has to make business sense. This is extra budget that the board has to approve.

There has to be a satisfactory return on investment (ROI) for my hours. That could be by reducing the audit fee and I usually insist on the external audit firm committing to a fee cut (or a reduced increase) that is clearly more than my cost. There can also be a side benefit, a reduction in management time, when the work is done by somebody who knows the business.

The Trainer hours were a combination of the two reasons. PwC's hours and fees were reduced, and we took some burden off management for explaining the company's systems, processes, and risks. When it came to checking the physical inventory in the refinery tank farm, my people didn't need the handholding necessary with junior PwC staff who had never done it before.

There are different ways to help the external auditors and it is up to the CAE to negotiate the best approach with them. My least preferred option is to lend them an auditor for a period to do "grunt" work, work that will not be enjoyed by my auditor nor enable them to learn.

I should mention that in one instance there was another consideration. One of my financial auditors was in the process of obtaining his CPA certification and needed to meet the requirement of a defined number of hours working under a CPA.

Before leaving this discussion, whether it is helping the external auditor by performing work they can rely on, or helping management by testing controls for SOX compliance, the CAE has to have sufficient resources to address the more significant risks to the enterprise!

Internal Audit's role in Sarbanes-Oxley Compliance

Helping management with their SOX compliance activities is somewhat similar in principle to performing work that the external auditor can rely on.

I will do it when I can fulfil all my other responsibilities and it is the right thing to do for the business.

One justification is that it reduces reliance on the external auditor when it comes to the adequacy of internal control over financial reporting because internal audit is testing all the key controls.

At Business Objects, EY told the audit committee that they had relied on testing performed by my team on behalf of management for 80% of the audit scope, reducing the audit fee by a million dollars.

The hours dedicated to the SOX compliance program are a line item in the audit plan.

Summary

Populating the audit plan with the right audit engagements to address the more significant sources of risk to enterprise objectives is as much an art as it is a science.

There are many options, and it requires experience and judgment.

Reviewing the draft audit plan with management and then with the Audit Committee can often be of great value. This is especially true when there is trust between management and internal audit, and management sees value in internal audit's work. By value, I mean value to management in running the business: assurance that things are as they should be, suggestions for constructive change, and other advice and insight.

I will discuss those reviews in chapter 9. Communicating the Audit Plan. But first, I want to talk about what goes in the audit plan.

8. What is in the Audit Plan?

"If you don't know where you are going, you'll end up someplace else." Yogi Berra

The audit plan is both a working document, in that its schedule of audits drives the work internal audit will perform, and a communications vehicle when descriptive text is included.

This chapter is about what should be included in the audit plan when it discussed and, hopefully, approved.

The content of the audit plan depends on what the CAE needs to communicate to satisfy the needs of the board (primarily) and management. In other words, what do they need to know?

- The board needs sufficient information to have reasonable assurance that internal audit is doing the work they will rely upon in their oversight of management performance, including risk management and internal control.

  The members will also want to know that internal audit will be able to provide them the assurance they need on the management of significant risks and the achievement of objectives.

  They will be concerned with the adequacy of internal audit resources as well as the competency of the team and its leader.

  In addition, the board should be concerned that internal audit is working effectively with the management team; this is something that reflects on both internal audit and management. I will highlight the engagements that have been requested by management and encourage the executives at the meeting to share their thoughts on the plan.

  The board needs to know whether this was accomplished in the prior year (the report with the audit plan normally includes a review of the prior year) as well as what will happen in the upcoming year.

The report with the audit plan usually includes budget vs. actual information, so the board can know that internal audit is financially responsible.

On occasion, the board wants to see additional information. At their request, I provided information in the Tosco audit plan in Appendix II on:

- Staff diversity and
- Staff certifications

- Management also wants to know that internal audit will provide it with the assurance it needs over the reliable performance of controls over the more significant risks.

Frequently, management is concerned about specific risks and looks to internal audit for both assurance and insights.

- Finally, management needs to know what internal audit will be doing so it can be prepared. Almost any audit engagement consumes management and staff attention and time.

Review of the Prior Year

All my audit plans start with a review of the prior period. I need to explain whether the work included in the plan shared with management and the Audit Committee as we started the year was completed – and if not, why not. In a dynamic environment and a continuously updated audit plan, they need to know how I and my team, with management input, determined what to do and when.

The Audit Committee usually ask management to comment on our work. Sometimes, they also ask the external auditors for their thoughts.

I also share any lessons learned and our performance against the budget given to me by the board.

This provides the context for the plans for the coming year. You can see examples in Appendices II and III.

Audit Strategy

If I am changing the approach from prior years, whether I was the CAE then or not, I need to explain that to management and the Audit Committee.

I have mentioned Solectron Corporation a few times and explained that I needed to change the audit approach to provide a greater level of assurance (and value) to my customers.

I have included in Appendix I a document I shared with top management and the Audit Committee as part of the plan for 2002, my first full year as CAE with the company.

Appendix II is the audit plan I shared with the Audit Committee of Tosco Corporation in my last year with them (I left when they were acquired by Phillips Petroleum.)

It includes my explanation of a shift in audit strategy from "controls auditing" to "controls assurance", something I intended to do through continuous auditing software that we would develop in 2001.

Appendix III has my audit plan for Business Objects. It includes information about the Software License Compliance function that had been added to my responsibilities in the previous year, and the Business Contingency Planning function that management wanted me to add[92].

Strategic Plan?

By the way, some people talk about a "strategic plan" for internal audit that covers some number of years. I don't believe in that. The world in which we live is too turbulent to believe that we can plan that far ahead. In addition, if a change in strategy is needed it should be completed as soon as possible, not over a period of years.

---

[92] Contingency planning was one of the areas I was responsible when I was a vice president in IT at two financial institutions.

If management has a longer term plan, I would consider whether I also need a longer term plan. For example, if management plans to expand into other countries in future years then I would have to think about how I would handle that.

What will we Audit?

I led both small and larger internal audit departments, from a staff of 3 to one of 50 people. When its length is manageable, I include a list of the engagements I plan to complete. But in the case of Tosco in 2000 we completed 199 internal audit projects – far too many to list. So, I provided in the audit plan other information on where and what we intended to audit – see Appendix II.

However, I always point out that we will continuously review and update the audit plan. I summarize the changes in each quarterly audit committee meeting.

9. Communicating the Audit Plan

"The single biggest problem in communication is the illusion that it has taken place." George Bernard Shaw

There are four steps in effectively communicating the audit plan:
1. Communicating and reviewing a draft *internally*
2. Communicating and reviewing a draft *with management*
3. Reviewing the risk assessment and plan with the external auditor
4. Reviewing the plan with the *Audit Committee*, and obtaining their approval

The Internal Review

It is easy to overlook the need to include the audit team in developing the audit plan. It is even easier to overlook the need to review it with them after it has been drafted.

This is especially important when there is a change in audit strategy.

The CAE needs his team, especially those in leadership positions or who have special skills he or she cannot afford to lose, to embrace the change.

Change management skills are needed to explain the change to the entire team and get them behind it.

Let us not forget that the CAE is only as good as his team. He or she may lead and set an example, but it is the team that performs the audits and delivers the results.

Reviewing the draft plan with the team can surface potential issues, for example whether there are potential obstacles that have been overlooked or a source of risk or opportunity that is greater than the CAE thought.

In a larger team, the CAE's direct reports are usually responsible for 'selling' the audit plan to local management. If they don't completely endorse and support it, the CAE will be in trouble.

The Review with Management

Earlier, I said:

> Management … wants to know that internal audit will provide it with the assurance it needs over the reliable performance of controls over the more significant risks.
>
> Frequently, management is concerned about specific risks and looks to internal audit for both assurance and insights.
>
> Finally, management needs to know what internal audit will be doing so it can be prepared. Almost any audit engagement consumes management and staff attention and time.

While the audit committee of the board is the primary customer for internal audit, management is also a customer.

Discussing the draft audit plan with management, not only top management but also those who lead different functions and business units, adds great value:

- It confirms that the risk assessment and that the planned audit engagements are the right ones to perform.

- It can highlight potential improvements in the plan, perhaps adding areas (such as a consulting engagement where management has recently decided to acquire and implement new software, or an assurance engagement where management has concerns) and/or deleting engagements where the risk or value has dropped (for example, where management has decided not to proceed with a planned project, or where management has re-assessed the level of risk and brought it down).

- Where the discussions with management help them see the value of the engagement, management has an element of "buy-in". Management can see that they have

- an opportunity to request internal audit work and otherwise affect what internal audit will be doing.
- It is also an opportunity to show management that internal audit is not trying to be the corporate police, but to help them and the organization be successful.
- Management can see how the audit plan will help them with assurance that the organization, systems, and processes they rely on are effective.
- Management can be prepared for the audit. They can ensure the people who will be involved are available, not on vacation or in training.

At a $28bn revenue company like Tosco, my team or I would discuss the draft audit plan with:

- The CFO
- General Counsel
- The two division CEOs
- The head of Shared Services
- The CIO
- The Corporate Controller
- The two division CFOs
- The Treasurer
- The vice president for refinery operations
- Each refinery manager
- The head of Corporate Environment, Health, and Safety
- The head of Information Security
- Several business unit and functional managers

I sent the audit plan to the CEO to see if he wanted to meet and discuss it, but he would reply that he trusted my judgment and the review by his management team.

After I or my director responsible for a division had met with the top division executives one-on-one, I would review the plan at a high level with each division's executive team in one of their regular meetings (which I or my director usually attended).

The CAE has the last word on what is in the plan, but a sensible CAE takes care to listen attentively to management's comments and suggestions.

The Review with the External Auditor

I consider this something of a desirable but optional step. Frankly, the external auditor in my experience showed little interest in the plan beyond what we were doing in support of SOX compliance.

However, a constructive conversation can have value, especially if the external auditor is willing to share more of their own risk assessment.

When the relationship with the external auditor is optimal, these discussions can lead to greater reliance by the external auditor on the work performed by internal audit.

Showing an interest in their work and exploring opportunities for collaboration (for example, when visiting a remote location or performing an inventory observation) will generally lead to a better relationship with the external auditor – which is useful any time there are serious control or financial reporting issues.

In addition, the Audit Committee will want to know that the audit plan has been discussed with both management and the external auditor. It gives credibility to the plan.

The Review with the Audit Committee

Nobody in attendance at the Audit Committee meeting, including management and the external auditor, should be surprised by the audit plan.

I like to send a draft to the members of the Audit Committee well in advance of the meeting where it will be approved. This is in addition to sending it with the meeting materials.

When I send the draft, I will not only ask for their comments but suggest a meeting or at least a call to discuss it.

This is especially true if I can anticipate problems, such as from budget limitations or a disagreement with management.

There is huge value if I can get the members' feedback and answer their questions before the meeting.

I don't want to have to justify the plan at the meeting or change it afterwards. I want the discussion at the meeting to be smooth, fast, and end with their approval.

A one-on-one review of the audit plan with each of the Audit Committee members, not just the chair, is an opportunity to:

- Discuss the business, the company's strategic plans, its risks, and its opportunities
- Build mutual trust and understanding
- Listen to their insights and advice
- Obtain their support, not only for this plan but for the future

As CAE, I acted as secretary for the chair in the Audit Committee meetings of each my companies. I worked with the chair and the members to agree on the schedule of meetings, each agenda, and record and/or approve the minutes.

My priorities in discussing the plan with the Audit Committee included:

- Obtain agreement that we have identified the more significant risks to the enterprise and that we have planned appropriate engagements to address them.
- Ensure we have the necessary budget and other resources.

- Provide them with assurance of the effectiveness of the internal audit function.

I believed then and still believe today that there are better ways to spend precious Audit Committee time than getting into the detail of the audit plan. Time discussing the audit plan can be minimized by diligently reviewing the plan and obtaining and addressing their comments *before* the meeting. The Audit Committee can then approve the audit plan quickly and move on to more important topics.

I have talked to other CAEs who say that their report to the Audit Committee takes 45-60 minutes. I took pride in keeping my report down to 15 minutes. The members of the committee had read and considered my report prior to the meeting, so I only had to highlight a few important points, confirm they had no questions, and ask for a vote to approve the plan.

10. Maintaining the Audit Plan

"Organizations are changing at warp speed. To keep up, internal audit needs to be agile, responsive, and focused on value delivery." Patricia Miller and Larry Rittenberg in Ia magazine[93], 2021

Continuous Risk Assessment

The world in which we live and work is changing all the time.

We need to audit what matters now and will matter tomorrow, rather than what *used to* matter at the beginning of the year, or even last week.

Working with a rigid annual audit plan that is probably out-of-date before it is approved by the Audit Committee makes little sense.

This was illustrated in the extreme when Business Objects S.A. (BOBJ), where I led both internal audit and risk management, announced that it was going to be acquired by SAP.

SAP was a far larger software company with a very different business model. While BOBJ had a high volume of relatively low orders, SAP had (in proportion) a lower volume of much larger contracts. In addition, the software maintenance contracts operated differently.

This would be SAP's largest acquisition by far.

SAP announced that they wanted BOBJ to operate semi-autonomously with some exceptions[94], and their CFO directed that BOBJ would have to move from the Oracle ERP systems to SAP's own within a year. This was much faster than SAP advised its customers.

Many of the top BOBJ individual performers were in the process of leaving the company and others were talking about their desire to

---

[93] The magazine of the global IIA
[94] BOBJ Internal audit and risk management would both be merged into SAP's functions at some point. However, the initial plan would be that I would lead an independent internal audit team for the first year or more, coordinating risk management activities with the SAP risk team.

find a new job. As noted earlier, the entire DBA team left quickly, as did the entire Credit department in the UK.

Clearly, there were significant risks to the success of the merger. They were more serious than anything else in our audit plan.

I believed then, and still believe today, that the possibility of the acquisition delivering less value than SAP had told the market was by far their greatest risk that year.

With the approval of the Business Objects Audit Committee (still in place) and top management, I tasked my entire team with helping management understand and address acquisition-related risks.

I also contacted my two counterparts at SAP: the senior vice president of GRC[95], who led risk management and other functions[96], and their CAE.

The head of GRC responded positively and promptly, assigning two of her best people to my team.

However, SAP's CAE refused to have any of his auditors work on the acquisition-related risks, including risks related to the systems migration. His reason was that it was not in the audit plan!

At each of my companies, over my 20-year career as CAE, I and my team continuously monitored the organization and its business context for changes in risk. (I should note that *management* is responsible for identifying new or changed risks, and we relied on them where we could.)

The Rolling Audit Plan

When I talk to management and the Audit Committee about the schedule of audits, I explain that while I may be pretty certain about what the team will work on over the next month or so, the further out the date the less certainty I have.

---

[95] Governance, risk management, and compliance.
[96] She was also responsible for SOX testing, information security management, and corporate policy management.

There's a precedent for this in financial management: rolling budgets and forecasts. This is one description[97] of rolling forecasts in the healthcare industry:

> Once a budget is created and approved, it begins degrading in usefulness as internal and external forces on a budget constantly change. In contrast, rolling forecasting is the process of reexamining financial information on a regular cadence to provide timely visibility into changing financials.
>
> Rolling forecasting enables healthcare leaders to update their financial projections on a monthly or quarterly basis to determine, "How has the previous month or quarter changed our view of the present and future?" It guides informed course corrections in response to current data and helps update near- and long-term projections. Rolling forecasting influences not only current expenditures and initiatives — such as ramping up traditional services at a time when consumers may avoid returning to a hospital setting — but also strategic decisions and future endeavors.
>
> The agility and visibility that rolling forecasting provides help healthcare leaders adjust strategy quickly as financial conditions change.

I adapted that concept and used a rolling audit plan or schedule.

Rather than trying to tell management that I would perform this or that audit more than three months ahead, I would share what I expected to audit over the next one to three months – indicating that there was uncertainty even three months out.

That doesn't mean that there was 100% certainty which audits my team would perform next. No. We believed in and practiced continuous risk assessment and plan maintenance, so we could always:

> Audit what matters for today and tomorrow

---

[97] From Syntellis, a vendor of financial planning solutions.

Continuous risk management

Unfortunately, it wasn't until late in my career that any of my companies had a risk management function. However, internal audit can (as mentioned earlier) leverage the work of the enterprise risk management activity if:

- It has been audited and assessed as reliable, and
- It is updated at an acceptable frequency

That latter point is important. If management only updates their risk assessment quarterly, that is better than annual but not sufficient in my opinion.

Risk doesn't wait until you are looking to change!

Continuous conversations

In Chapter 5, I discussed talking to (more accurately, listening to) executives and others as part of our risk assessment activity.

This is something that should be more continuous. It should not be an annual activity.

Like many CAEs, I designated members of my team as points of contact with various members of management or to monitor specific areas of risk. For example, my direct reports at Tosco met with management of their areas of responsibility on at least a monthly basis, if not more often. They built relationships with executives including:

- The CEO and Controller (or CFO) of their division and most of their direct reports
- The CIO and some of his direct reports
- The head of Shared Services
- The head of Environmental, Health, and Safety Compliance[98]
- The vice president responsible for operations

---

[98] One of my direct reports was a certified environmental auditor.

- Each refinery manager
- The head of our commodity trading operations

I had continuing conversations with most of the same people. However, my meetings with the division CEOs and Controllers were less frequent as I would only meet when I was in that location.

Of course, I also met with the corporate officers as often as I could, some more frequently than others. For example, I met with the Corporate Controller at least once each month (plus frequent lunches) but my discussions with General Counsel, the corporate CFO, and the corporate CEO tended to be when I visited the corporate offices in Connecticut[99].

Listening to the executives is not enough. Their view from 30,000 ft. is not always consistent with what is happening on the ground.

I like to get into the field and talk to/listen to as many people as I could.

I would strike up a conversation with refinery operations staff, the manager of a convenience store, or anybody else who could tell me about their job – and especially their challenges.

There's a concept in management science of "managing by walking around". This is one explanation[100]:

> The concept of management by walking around emerged back in the early 80s, 1982 to be specific when Tom Peters and Robert Waterman introduced it in their book named "In Search of Excellence". Peters and Waterman had followed

---

[99] The corporate offices were separate from the headquarters of the operating divisions. Only the top corporate officers were in Connecticut while Refining management was in New Jersey and Marketing in Arizona. The Corporate Controller, CIO, and head of Shared Services were also in Arizona.
[100] From *Leadership Ahoy!* The piece is written by Carl Lindberg, a CEO. I recommend the article at https://www.leadershipahoy.com/management-by-walking-around-explained-by-a-ceo/.

successful leaders and concluded that they did not stay in their "ivory towers" but instead spent time out in the organization, walking around the area and interacting with employees.

Management by walking around, otherwise known as management by wandering around (MBWA), is a management style that involves strolling around the work area in a seemingly unstructured manner. Managers spontaneously stop for a conversation with employees, learning more about equipment, functions, and processes in the workplace. As a manager stops by for informal discussions, she also makes herself available for employees and any questions they might want to raise. This approach builds participation and is an example of the democratic leadership style.

In a conversation I had with Tom Peters[101], he agreed with my suggestion that MBWA should be changed to "managing by *listening* around".

One example of MBWA led to a very valuable audit engagement.

Every so often, I would arrange to spend several hours with one of the convenience store (Circle K brand) district managers. Each district manager was responsible for several individual Circle K stores, many of which also sold gasoline and diesel, generally branded Union 76[102].

---

[101] We follow each other on Twitter, which is where the conversation happened.
[102] Tosco acquired the Circle K stores and then, after the subsequent acquisition of the Unocal Inc. gas stations and refineries, relabeled most of their gas pumps as Union 76, the Unocal brand. Tosco also had gas stations in the Northeast of the US that were branded as Exxon.

I would do a "ride-along" with the district manager, visiting several stores where I would chat with the store manager and staff, and listen to the district manager as he was driving between them.

On one of these trips, the district manager told me that he found it very hard to work with the "corporate" office (he was referring to Tosco Marketing division, which ran the Circle K business). He portrayed it as an "ivory tower" where the executives had lost touch with the business[103].

While that gave me something to think about, he shared something more tangible to address.

One of his store managers was notified that the city of Phoenix was going to perform major roadwork that would disrupt his business for several weeks. His store was on one corner of a very busy city intersection, with two other gas stations on other corners. The work would block access to all three stations' pumps and a major part of his revenue would be lost.

The manager had a great idea!

He submitted the paperwork requesting capital funds to build a new on-ramp to his gas pumps, bypassing the roadwork. The few thousand dollars investment would have a massive return: not only would his store continue to service existing customers during the roadwork, but commuters using the intersection on their way to and from downtown would probably switch to his service station. Those commuters might decide to stay with us long-term.

Unfortunately, it took months for the request for capital to be approved, by which time the roadwork had been completed and the opportunity lost.

I took this back to the executives in the corporate office, and they told me that the capital approval process always took far longer than it

---

[103] While the division CEO routinely stopped in the stores to chat, few of his management team did – unless they needed to buy something.

should because multiple approvals were needed; even the CEO got involved and had to review and approve *every* capital request.

This led to an audit of the capital approval process that not only resolved the bottleneck but identified the root cause, which my auditor discussed one-on-one with the division CEO. He realized that his difficulty in delegating decisions like this was something he had to change.

This one audit, performed as a result of listening while walking (or driving) around changed the culture of the organization.

Some years later, when I was CAE at Business Objects, I was in our London office to meet with the executives and listen to them share their insights on the business.

One of my meetings was with the manager of the Legal team; they were responsible for providing legal advice to the executive team. They also had a major role in the revenue process. In a software company, all potential deals must be reviewed by Legal before any revenue can be recognized (required by revenue recognition rules).

The attorney told me that he and the other members of his team, another attorney and a paralegal, were brutally overworked. They were working more hours than they should just to keep up with the flow of revenue deals for their review.

I asked him about his ability to provide legal advice to the executive team and he admitted that he was usually too busy. Most of the executives, including the local CEO, were using outside counsel for the advice.

He was not involved in selecting those legal firms and didn't know whether the executives were getting good advice or not. His body language communicated his unspoken concern that the legal advice was not as good as it should have been.

I confirmed this with the local CEO and my team performed an audit a couple of months later. They used analytics to understand the flow of revenue deals and were able to suggest how Legal's contract review workload could be reduced without incurring much more risk.

Essentially, the level of review would vary depending on the size of the deal and other factors.

Neither of these valuable audits were in the audit plan I discussed with management and the board as we started the year.

> "I was active in Raytheon's Diversity efforts and was the executive champion for several years. This gave me the opportunity to meet with our Employee Resource Groups where I learned much about where the fires were, where we had risk, and how internal audit could add more value. That came about because they trusted me – there are lots of ways to "listen" as you say to many within the organization with great information if they trust sharing with you. When the chair of the Audit Committee asked me why I wanted to assist the company as Diversity Champion, I explained how it helped me build trust, brand and insight. He said he never would have thought about

Continuous monitoring

There are other ways to stay abreast of changing business conditions, both internally and externally. For example:

- I reviewed the monthly financial results and forecasts for each of the company's business units, as well as the consolidated results. I paid attention to significant variances as they could be indicators of control or risk management issues.
- I attended the monthly meetings of the executive teams (and my direct reports did the same) and listened. I followed up with individual members of management on issues that came up.
- The CFO's quarterly review of the operating and financial results for the last quarter and forecast for the next quarter and remainder of the year was an excellent source.
- I received and reviewed many of the reports used by management in running the business, from financial reports to operational reports. For example, I received reports on

personnel changes, with special attention to the loss of executives or individuals in key financial reporting roles.

- As mentioned earlier, at some companies we used our own analytics to understand what was happening and highlight changes of significance.
- I often joined other company employees for lunch and listening. Some former members of the internal audit team had moved into management, and they were usually a good source of information as well.
- I benchmarked what we were doing against other companies in the same industry. For example, there was a group of CAEs in the oil industry that met from time to time. Larry Harrington of Raytheon used to read the company's competitors' filings with the SEC
- I subscribed to trade journals and other sources of information about the business.
- My door was always open, and all levels of management and staff used it from time to time.[104]

In addition, I networked with other CAEs, listen to them at conferences, and follow them on social media for ideas.

Changing and communicating the rolling audit plan

It is one thing to know that risks and opportunities are changing.

It is another to change the audit plan and schedule[105].

---

[104] One of the most wonderful moments was when a staff accountant came in to ask me why my team was the only group that seemed to enjoy their work!

[105] Earlier, I explained that the audit plan presented to the Audit Committee had a number of sections, only one of which was the schedule of audits. In practice, only the schedule and the budget vs. actual financials are updated continuously.

© Norman Marks, 2022, all rights reserved

I recall sitting down in New Jersey with my audit director, for the East Coast Refining business, Tom. One of his team was about to finish an audit and I asked Tom what he was going to work on next.

Tom looked at the audit schedule and told me what it said was the next audit. I replied:

> "We all need to learn that auditing the right things, but at the wrong time, is as ineffective as not auditing the right things or auditing the wrong things."
>
> Larry Harrington

"Yes, that is the next audit on the schedule. But what is the *right* audit to do next?"

We then had a constructive discussion, taking into account what we had learned through our recent listening around.

I had Tom and my other direct reports share with their respective customers what we had planned for the upcoming three months. But we also told them that we would revisit it constantly and welcomed their input.

The further out the schedule, the more likely it might change.

One of the challenges was the need to re-balance the audit plan as we completed audits, as well as removed, changed, or added engagements.

I worked with Tom to build an Excel model that always told him whether he would have the resources to complete what was now planned, or whether he had more resources than anticipated because audits were completed early.

Working with top management and the Audit Committee

When I started at each company, both top management and the Audit Committee were used to a fixed audit plan. They had worked with CAEs who would tell them precisely which audits would be performed in which month.

My approach was totally different.

In today's parlance, I would call it *agile* auditing[106].

When I explained my approach, everybody agreed it simply made sense. They approved of the idea that we were always looking to see where we could add most value, recognizing that the business and its environment were constantly changing.

The annual audit plan supported my budget and gave them an indication of where I saw we could add value through audit engagements.

But every quarter, I would share with them not only progress against plan but how I had changed it since the last meeting. It was usually easy to explain projects I added, and the more interesting discussions were about the reasons I had taken audits off the schedule.

In the Tosco audit plan shown in Appendix II, I reported that we had been:

> Working with management to continuously update our risk assessment and audit plan. This has resulted in changing a number of internal audits to address key business needs. For example, we worked with management to ensure the revenue system was billing all sales and that inventory was fairly stated; we are completing operational flowcharts as part of an audit of terminal billings to reduce the risk inherent in moving the function from Bayway to Phoenix; and we completed two consulting projects for the CFO and one for the CEO of the Marketing division (TMC).

In the Business Objects plan included in Appendix II, I reported:

> Acknowledged best practice is for internal audit work to be aligned with business risks, which change continuously. As a result, world-class internal audit organizations develop an audit plan that is flexible, based on a continuously updated assessment of business risk.
>
> The plan presented here is an approximation based on today's knowledge of the projects that are likely to be

---

[106] Being agile, rather than adhering to the Agile methodology.

completed in 2008. The schedule will be updated on a regular basis.

Should the schedule of work change significantly, for example as we know more about SAP's plans, an update will be provided to the Audit Committee.

While some believe that a measure of internal audit excellence is completion of the annual audit plan, I see that as an indicator of ineffectiveness.

Continuous audit planning, based on continuous risk assessment (including listening around), enables an internal audit team to perform:

Audits that matter
When they matter, and
Provide valuable information for those running the business

Continuous audit planning and the annual audit plan

One of the objections I have heard about continuous audit planning is that it will consume too much time that should be spent on auditing.

The people raising the objection believe that it means that they would perform as much work every month as they currently do once a year for the annual plan.

The answer is that when you adopt a continuous audit planning methodology, you just roll into the annual plan. You are constantly looking ahead, anticipating what might happen and which projects you should do.

All that needs to be done is to extend your vision to the end of the next year, then update the budget and put your annual plan document together.

In other words, the time spent at the end of the year is much *less* than if you follow a rigid annual planning approach.

It is true that audit planning time across the year is increased. But then the value provided by internal audit is significantly more as well.

We are providing the *actionable* information that they need and value, when they need it, to leaders of the organization.

I am encouraged that more and more internal audit functions are updating their audit plan more and more frequently. Some have only moved to quarterly, while others are monthly.

I prefer continuous.

The business is run every day.

Decisions are made every day.

Let's align with what the business needs, when it needs it.

That requires continuous reassessment and agile realignment of the audit plan.

Closing Thoughts

"Governance, risk management, compliance, assurance and audit professionals need to be innovative in what they do and how they do it to evolve from a <u>hindsight</u> perspective where they traditionally reported on the past, to delivering <u>insights</u> that help business managers now, and ultimately, they need to share <u>foresight</u> that helps business managers run the business in the future."

Bruce Turner (audit committee chair) in CERM Insights, 2021

The IIA has developed and shared *Core Principles for the Professional Practice of Internal Auditing*[107]. It includes some key words that Bruce Turner used in that article (with my highlights).

> The Core Principles, taken as a whole, articulate internal audit effectiveness. For an internal audit function to be considered effective, all Principles should be present and operating effectively. How an internal auditor, as well as an internal audit activity, demonstrates achievement of the Core Principles may be quite different from organization to organization, but failure to achieve any of the Principles would imply that an internal audit activity was not as effective as it could be in achieving internal audit's mission.
>
> - Demonstrates integrity.
> - Demonstrates competence and due professional care.
> - Is objective and free from undue influence (independent).
> - Aligns with the strategies, objectives, and risks of the organization.
> - Is appropriately positioned and adequately resourced.
> - Demonstrates quality and continuous improvement.

---

[107] Available on their website. I was a member of the task force that developed the principles.

- Communicates effectively.
- Provides risk-based assurance.
- Is insightful, proactive, and future-focused.
- Promotes organizational improvement.

They are not organized in priority order as all are deemed essential.

The last three relate to the valued services provided by internal audit to the organization, so are highly relevant to this book.

The first of these three is *"provides risk-based assurance"*.

When we operate from a continuously updated audit plan, we are *focusing on the risks that matter*. We will choose between assurance and consulting engagements, but the overall intent is to help the organization have reliable processes, systems, organization, and controls so they can be effective in managing risks and achieving enterprise objectives.

The second is that internal audit *"Is insightful, proactive, and future-focused"*.

When we continually strive to focus on current risks, with an eye to the future, we are certainly *future-focused*. We can also be *proactive* in addressing what might become an issue.

The last is a given. We are not paid to find problems, but to help the organization succeed.

We do that by providing decision-makers and leaders of the organization with actionable assurance, advice, and insight that is relevant to the issues of the day.

While the IIA has a short set of core principles, mine (which I stated at the beginning of the book) are a little longer and more detailed. Here they are again, with additional discussion this time. (These are not necessarily in order of significance. All are important.)

1. **Provide the Audit Committee and management with the *assurance, advice*, and *insight* they need *on what matters now and will matter in the future* to the success of the business.**

   Interpretation

   There are several points here:

   - Our primary service is assurance (providing peace of mind that the organization of the enterprise, its processes, systems, people, and controls can be relied upon).
   - We also provide advice and insight so that the organization can continue to upgrade its processes, etc., *even when they are not yet broken!*
   - We should not be auditing the controls that operated in the past. *We should be auditing the controls and their effectiveness in managing the risks of today and tomorrow.*
   - In order to do that, we need an agile plan that is continuously updated.

2. **Provide the *actionable* information they need *when* they need it.**

   Interpretation

   When there is a need to make corrective actions, we need to express ourselves clearly so that management and the board can take the necessary steps.

   We <u>must</u> communicate promptly with management so that those necessary steps can be taken promptly. Delays in communication mean that exposures remain longer.

3. **Be *agile* and *efficient* in both planning and execution of every audit engagement.**

Interpretation

- Agile planning is the topic of this book
- We have to be efficient as we every wasted hour is an hour that could have been used on a valuable audit engagement.
- As I explain in *Auditing that Matters*, the work should stop when enough has been done to form an opinion and the cost of continuing exceeds any value to the organization.
- However, we should not be constrained by the engagement budget when significant value is added by going over the budget.

4. *Focus* **on what matters and exclude from scope anything that does not matter.**

Interpretation

As explained in this book and in *Auditing that Matters*, audit what matters to the achievement of enterprise objectives. *Don't audit an area or process where, if controls failed, they wouldn't have a significant effect on the achievement of enterprise objectives.*

5. **Write (and otherwise communicate) for the time-limited, speed-reading executive. Don't waste anybody's time but get the message across and drive action!**

Interpretation

This is also covered in *Auditing that Matters*. We need to communicate effectively and that means excluding anything from either written or oral reports that our customer doesn't need to read.

Get to the point and stop. Don't bury value in a mass of trivial detail.

6. **Work** *with* **management to ensure they can rely on their processes, systems, organization, and controls as they direct and manage the company to achieve its objectives.**

Interpretation

We share management and the board's goal: the success of the organization. We should not allow the principle of 'independence' to get in the way of the practice of helping the organization succeed.

7. **Measure the success of internal audit by the success of the company, not by the number of audits performed or the number of issues identified.**

    ### Interpretation

    No interpretation is required.

8. **Recognize that quality and effectiveness are best recognized through the eyes of the satisfied customer.**

    ### Interpretation

    The opinion of our customer is the only metric that really matters.

I hope the discussion and stories in this book help you develop and then maintain the kind of audit plan that will help your team perform world-class internal audit services for your organization.

The three appendices are examples of audit plans that show how I practiced internal auditing over my career.

Appendix I: Solectron Audit Strategy

I have mentioned how I needed to change the internal audit approach when I took over as Vice President, Internal Audit of Solectron in 2001.

Solectron (SLR) was an electronics contract manufacturing company for companies like Apple, IBM, Hewlett-Packard, Dell, Nortel, Nokia, Cisco, Lucent, Motorola, and others.

In 2001, its revenue was $17,437 million but it recorded a loss from continuing operations of $124 million. Although it had in prior years experienced rapid growth (from $9,669 million revenue in 1999) and reasonable profits, its margins were thin and, in some places, negative.

A serious issue at almost any location could be material to its ability to earn value for its shareholders.[108]

I used the following as part of the audit plan, describing the new approach and how it differed from what the company was used to.

The acronyms used are:

- CSA: control self-assessment, as described in the text.
- A&F: Solectron had an Audit and Finance committee with the same responsibilities as a traditional Audit Committee plus oversight of the Finance function.

A "site" was one of the more than one hundred factories the company owned and operated around the world. They were primarily assembly plants, but a few manufactured components.

---

[108] What I would consider to be management failures led to the decline of Solectron until it was sold to its major competitor, Flextronics, in 2007 for $3.6 billion. (I left the company in 2004.)

PRINCIPLE	CURRENT	ACTION
1. Provide assurance to the Audit & Finance Committee (A&F) that processes are in place to effectively manage business risks.	In 2001, performed 17 site audits, 4 process/function audits, and 5 special projects. This is not sufficient to provide assurance on total system of internal controls.	In 2002, extend CSA program to have all sites self-assess every year. IA will perform a combination of desk and field reviews to confirm self-assessments selectively. Perform more audits of processes and business risk management that extend beyond a single site.
	Not involved in new systems projects except after the fact. Limited contribution to assurance of their success. After-the-fact audits are reporting, not assuring.	Become proactively involved in controls and security assurance of new systems, policies, and processes.
	IT risks addressed at sites, and to limited depth.	Risk-assess IT issues, and partner with co-sourcing firm to extend IT audit resources.

2.	Provide objective appraisals to A&F and management of controls over critical business functions and processes.	Appraisals are objective. However, not all critical business risks are addressed. Focus is on major and new sites, and a few processes.	Perform more audits of processes and business risk management that extend beyond a single site.
3.	Work proactively with management to ensure changes do not introduce more than acceptable risks.	Not involved in new systems projects except after the fact. Limited contribution to assurance of their success.	Become proactively involved in controls and security assurance for new systems, policies, and processes.
4.	Communicate appraisals and counsel effectively and efficiently.	Average audit report exceeds 50 pages. Executive summary is a dozen pages or more.	Break down report into 2 sections: a report with no more than 2 pages (unless there are issues requiring executive management attention); and a detailed action plan package. Issue each only to those who need them.

		Scorecard approach highlights the importance of issues **at site or process materiality levels**. However, the reports do not indicate whether the issues are significant to senior or executive management.	Include in the report an assessment of whether issues require attention beyond site level.
		Assessments do not consistently show context – whether matters are improving, etc. Concern whether reports are balanced.	Ensure all assessments are balanced, emphasizing positive as well as negative, and are in context.
5.	Operate on business principles. Perform work that is cost/value justified. Develop talent for the future. Manage costs.	Average CSA cost is currently in excess of $100,000 plus travel. Credit card audit had a team of 9 people.	Reduce scope and size of typical audit field review of CSAs. Perform desk reviews of all CSA and field reviews selectively. Size audits based on cost: value/risk. Perform more solo, shorter audits that focus selectively on risks.
		Average audit report exceeds 50 pages.	Reduce audit report size as described above.

		Staff does not have many stars for the future.	Counsel non-performing staff. Do not hire average performers, and co-source when top performers not available.
		Budget out of date before year starts.	Update 2002 budget.
6.	Contribute to the continuing quality improvement of risk management processes and internal control systems.	The CSAs are effective in promoting the understanding and ownership by site management of internal controls and SLR's expectations and policies.	Extend the CSAs to all sites, every year.
		Controls training and orientation outside the CSA process is limited.	Provide early controls training and orientation to every new site.

7.	Function as staff and counsel to A&F on their Audit Committee functions. Help A&F ensure all required Audit Committee tasks are performed, that they are informed of the nature of business risks as they change, and manage the agenda.	CAE participates in agenda definition. Agenda is not laid out, for full year, to ensure all appropriate discussions are held (e.g., annual review of committee charter, committee self-assessment, briefing by Ethics Officer, Security Officer, and Legal Counsel, etc.) Audit portion of each A&F meeting is limited. No discussion of key risks, no management presentations.	Develop recommended calendar and discuss with A&F chair.
8.	Perform other projects that add value (in excess of cost).	A limited number of projects are performed (e.g., duplicate payments review).	Search for opportunities (e.g., contracts audit).

Appendix II: Tosco Audit Plan

In the text, I have shared excerpts from the audit plan (schedule of planned audits) for the Bayway refinery and related activities. The text below is the consolidated audit plan I shared with top management and the Audit Committee.

The Year in Review and Plans for 2001[109]

I. Introduction

As I did last year, this document discusses my business plan in some depth. In order to minimize meeting time, I plan to review only the highlights in the Audit Committee meeting and answer any questions.

II. The Year in Review

This has been a successful year for the department. Highlights include:

- Completing 183 internal audit projects, a few less than were completed in 1999 and are planned for 2001.

- Working with management to continuously update our risk assessment and audit plan. This has resulted in changing a number of internal audits to address key business needs. For example, we worked with management to ensure the revenue system was billing all sales and that inventory was fairly stated; we are completing operational flowcharts as part of an audit of terminal billings to reduce the risk inherent in moving the function from Bayway[110] to Phoenix[111]; and, we completed two consulting projects for the CFO and one for the CEO of the Marketing division (TMC).

- In a period of abnormally high demand for internal auditors (especially with IT skills), we kept our staff turnover at a

---

[109] The plan has been modified to remove personal names, etc.
[110] A Tosco refinery in New Jersey and the HQ of the Refining division (TRC)
[111] The HQ of the Marketing division (TMC) and shared services (TSS)

© Norman Marks, 2022, all rights reserved

reasonable level. We filled all open positions relatively quickly, with the exception of a delay in one IT auditor position (now filled). Much of this is due to our leading-edge approach to internal auditing.

- Customer satisfaction remains high. A survey during the year indicated that almost all of customers believe our audits add value to their operations. In all areas, we worked effectively with management to avoid problems in new systems and correct any that we found in existing systems. We have not been denied access to any information, people, or other resources.

- Our major change objectives for the year were achieved (addressing the new issues surrounding e-business; integrating the new Project Quality Assurance function into the new self-directed IT audit work team; and adopting some new tools and techniques). We also achieved our EEO hiring goals for the year.

- This was another successful year for Contracts Audit, with significant savings for the company.

- Good progress was made by Audit Investigations in implementing a fraud detection program. They also had a productive year in terms of investigations.

- Costs were within budget.

- Working with the Audit Committee as it adapts to the recommendations of the Blue Ribbon Committee. Continuing to chair and to provide leadership to the Business Ethics Committee[112].

- We remained active in the profession. I am active at the international level, had an article published, and edit a new column in the Institute of Internal Auditor's magazine. I have been asked to be a speaker at a major conference next Spring. The leader of our Marketing division audit team is the President of the Phoenix chapter of the IIA.

---

[112] I was nominally (according to filings with the SEC) the company's Ethics Officer.

Staffing

As discussed above, we had a reasonable level of turnover.

1. Internal audit turnover of 8% is down compared to the 18% in 1999 and prior years. We lost one auditor to an internal transfer (desired) and one to an opportunity outside the company.
2. Contracts audit turnover was higher. We lost a contracts auditor to a transfer, laid one off as a result of the Avon[113] sale, and two others left the company.

While we see, by design, people leave the department after 2-3 years, our turnover rate is very reasonable compared to other companies. The charts included below are from a recent study (GAIN) by the Institute of Internal Auditors (in 2000 for 1999 data) and reflect internal audit activity only.

STAFF TURNOVER RATE

We continue to hire predominantly experienced personnel; we have become known within the company as a good place to work and have attracted a large number of internal applicants.

---

[113] A Tosco refinery in Northern California

Auditing at the Speed of Risk with an Agile, Continuous Audit Plan

AVERAGE STAFF EXPERIENCE

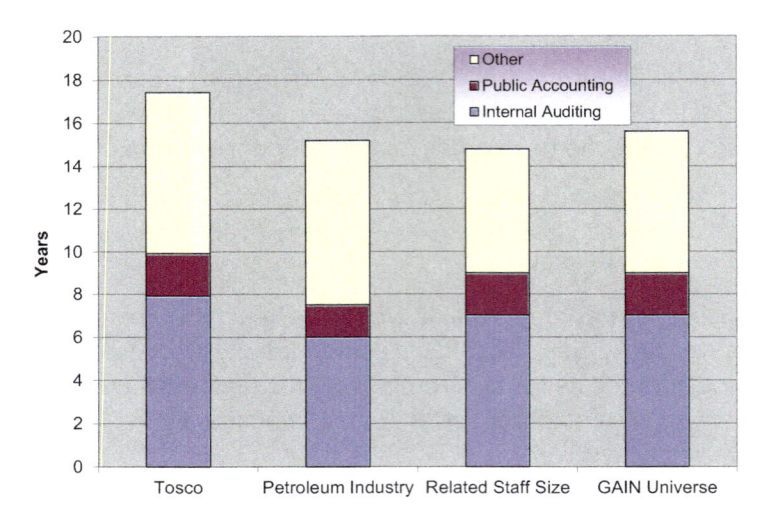

While we do not require (as do many others) a CPA, CIA, CISA, or other certification, most have at least one and frequently several professional credentials. The percentage of credentialed employees is down from 95% last year.

PERCENTAGE OF STAFF WITH PROFESSIONAL DESIGNATIONS

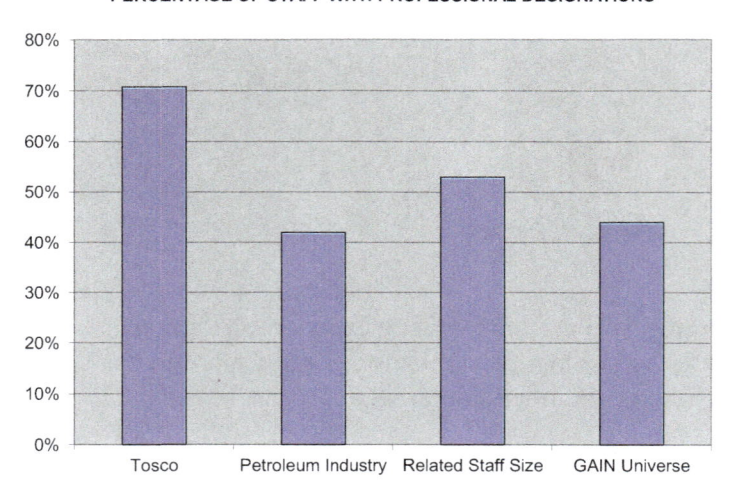

We were successful in identifying talented minority staff and met our hiring goals for the year. We remain committed to diversity in every respect, especially in experience and perspective.

		Female	Total Black[2]	Total Hispanic[2]	Total A/PI[2]	Total AI[2]
November '97[1]	Count	4	0	1	1	0
	%	16.0%	0.0%	4.0%	4.0%	0.0%
November '98[1]	Count	6	0	1	2	0
	%	19.4%	0.0%	3.2%	6.5%	0.0%
November '99[1]	Count	10	0	1	3	0
	%	33.3%	0.0%	3.3%	10.0%	0.0%
November '00[1]	Count	11	2	2	2	0
	%	29.7%	5.4%	6.7%	5.4%	0.0%
Availability[3,4]	%	25.1%	3.8%	2.2%	2.9%	1.7%
2001 Goal: add		0	0	0	0	0

Notes:

(1) Statistics include all auditors, from both internal and contracts audit, excluding the General Auditor[114] and assistants

(2) Categories are: Black, Hispanic, Asian/Pacific Islanders, and American Indian.

(3) Source for total female auditors: "The Internal Auditor Job Market 1996", Institute of Internal Auditors

---

[114] That was my title as CAE.

Internal Audit

We completed approximately the same number of audits (183) as in the schedule provided to the Committee last year. As usual, we have adapted our schedule of audits as business conditions, risks, and values change.

We have not had to defer or cancel any planned audits of major risk areas, with the obvious exception of the Avon refinery. However, we have changed several audits from the traditional to a more value-added approach. In particular, we have dedicated significant resources to assisting refinery accounting obtain assurance that inventory, receivables, and sales are properly stated.

The Retail Enterprise Project[115] and the various e-commerce initiatives have been major priorities throughout the year. I believe we have added significant value through our proactive controls consulting, as well as our involvement on the project Steering Committees.

Our work at Wood River and Alliance[116] has been restricted to controls consulting. A complete program of audits will start in 2001.

Finally, we completed two major consulting projects for the CFO on the revenue system and the Refining division closing process. At the time of writing, we are preparing to complete a consulting project for the Marketing CEO on negotiation effectiveness.

Financial controls audits continue to be the emphasis of the department. We believe this is in line with business risks, where our resources can provide most value, and where we can meet our customers' needs (primarily those of the Audit Committee).

As I have reported in the past, we are considered in the profession to be a best practice, leading-edge, internal audit group. A recent study (see separate section) by Dr. James Roth described the features of a "value-adding audit department". While he did not review Tosco per se, he could be describing us. Arthur Andersen will be profiling Tosco Audit as one of a handful of best practices internal audit functions they include in their (subscription) benchmarking website.

---

[115] A massive investment in new software that included new devices and software in every store as well as new systems in the Marketing HQ.
[116] Newly acquired refineries near, respectively, St. Louis and New Orleans

NUMBER AND TYPE OF AUDITS 1991-2000

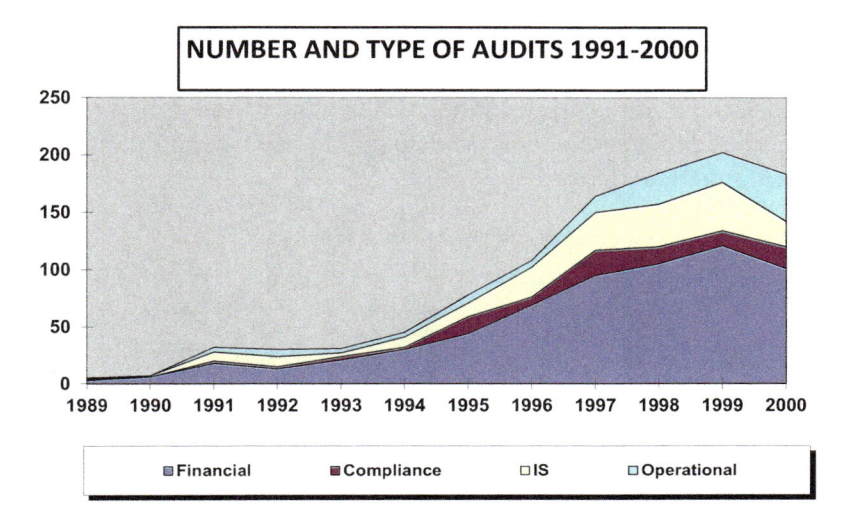

(Chart showing stacked area data from 1989 to 2000 with categories: Financial, Compliance, IS, Operational. Y-axis ranges from 0 to 250.)

Contracts Audit

This has been another solid year.

In Refining, we were busy supporting a number of turnaround projects. The greater part of the value on these projects is typically through a combination of pre-turnaround contract consulting (e.g., assisting with price and terms negotiation) and a visible presence during the turnarounds themselves. Our work also includes a post-turnaround review of billings. That work at Avon recovered $851,000 alone. In addition, we avoided $572,000 in Avon charges that should have been billed to UDS[117].

As I reported last year, we have refocused our efforts on preventing unnecessary expenditures by proactive consulting rather than recovering excess payments made. We have been heavily involved in the contracts for the polypropylene plant and the co-generation upgrade at Bayway. This approach has the effect of limiting the hard dollars saved but increasing total value to the company. In addition, we are able to work more effectively, in a less confrontational mode, with operating management.

---

[117] The company that acquired the Avon refinery from Tosco

In Phoenix, we continue to perform almost exclusively audits to verify billings and recover overcharges. Audits of cigarette vendors have been especially fruitful (approximately $900,000). In addition, we have continued to audit vendors who appear to have inappropriate relationships with employees.

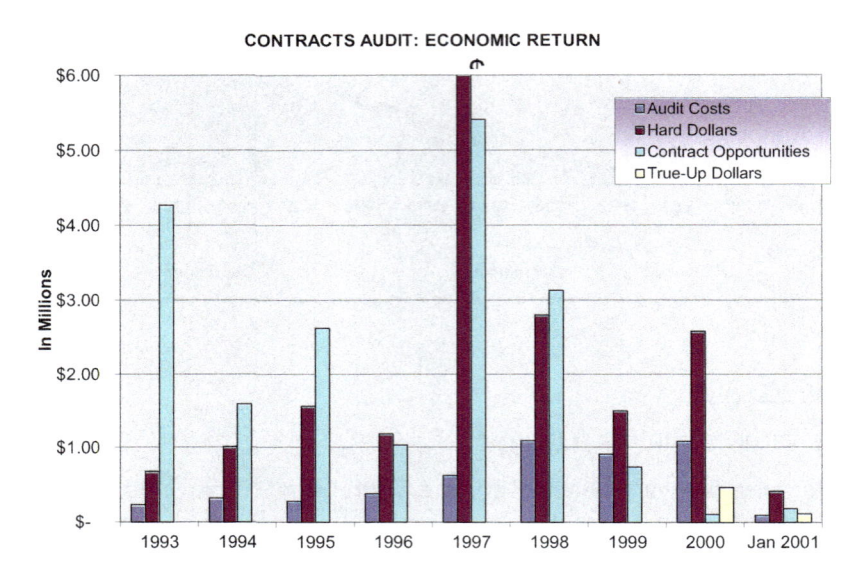

CONTRACTS AUDIT: ECONOMIC RETURN

Audit Investigations

As discussed privately with the Audit Committee, this has been another busy year. While we continue to uncover inappropriate activity, we are working effectively with management to improve detective controls and training to reduce future incidence.

Budget vs. Actual Costs

We finished the year under budget. The favorable variance in refining is because we decided not to use all the outsourcing money and have not added staff as rapidly as planned in Wood River and Alliance. In marketing, we were over budget because we put more IT Audit emphasis on e-business initiatives.

	TRC		TMC/TSS		Corporate		TOTAL	
	Budget	Actual	Budget	Actual	Budget	Actual	Budget	Actual
Internal Audit	1,634	1,530	1,066	1,241	563	645	3,263	3,415
Contracts Audit	919	719	446	357			1,365	1,077
TOTAL	2,553	2,249	1,512	1,598	563	645	4,628	4,492

We continue to be a low-cost leader. Our internal audit costs as a percentage of net sales remain significantly below industry and profession averages.

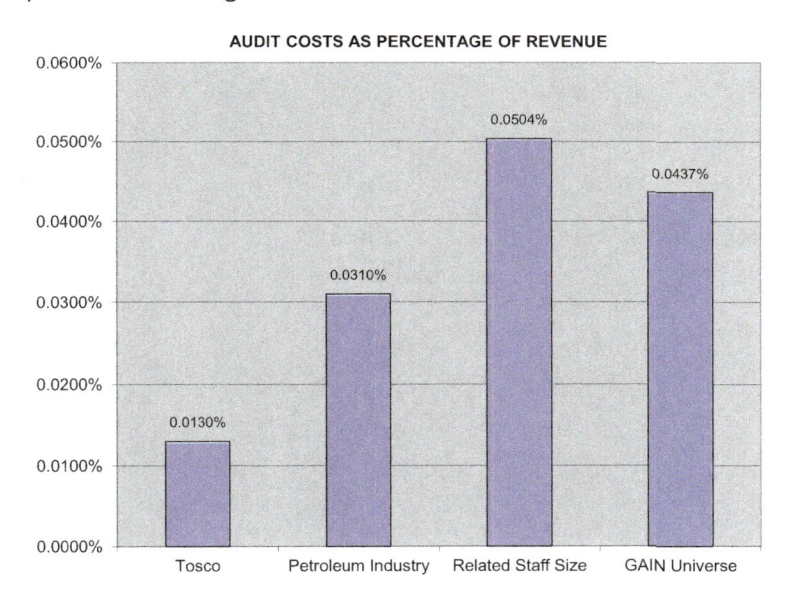

AUDIT COSTS AS PERCENTAGE OF REVENUE

Tosco	0.0130%
Petroleum Industry	0.0310%
Related Staff Size	0.0504%
GAIN Universe	0.0437%

The next chart shows our cost trend over the last several years. The dip in 2000 and 2001 reflects, in part, the effect of higher crude prices. However, there is an underlying reduction in our costs. They have grown much more slowly than the company. But I remain comfortable that I can address the company's major business risks with this level of resources and understand that I have the approval of the Audit Committee and the CFO to add staff if necessary to address critical areas.

Auditing at the Speed of Risk with an Agile, Continuous Audit Plan

INTERNAL AUDIT COSTS AS A PERCENTAGE OF NET SALES

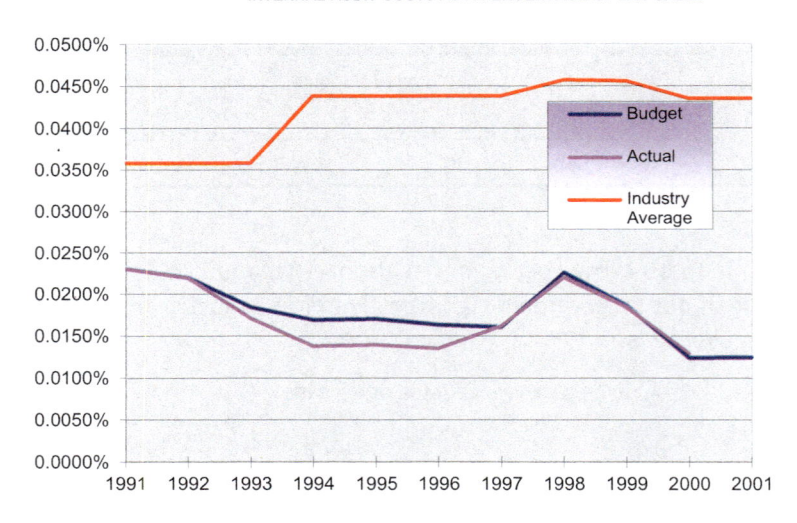

We also are a leader in employees per auditor.

EMPLOYEES PER AUDITOR

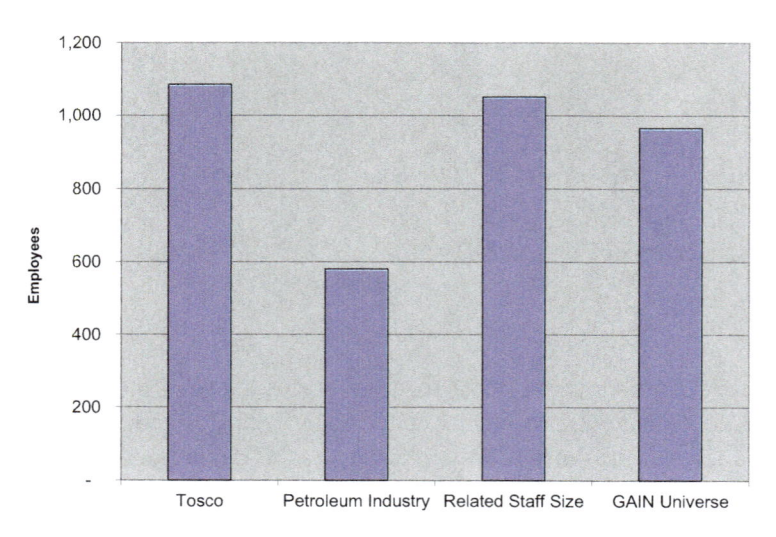

2001

My change initiatives for the next year include:

Auditing at the Speed of Risk with an Agile, Continuous Audit Plan

- Making the philosophical move from "controls auditing" to "controls assurance". Instead of relying on periodic audits, we will (where it is both practical and cost-effective) start monitoring controls performance on a more continuous basis. This is likely to include partnering with existing monitoring groups within the company, such as refining's Loss Prevention function and the Corporate Safety, Health and Environment department. The goal is to provide higher quality assurance to the Audit Committee and senior management on controls adequacy and performance, preferably without increasing cost.
- Establishing internal and contracts audit functions at Wood River and Alliance.
- Providing more of a coordinated focus on audits of safety, health, and environmental risks, working closely with the corporate Safety, Health, and Environmental Compliance (S, H, & E) group. This will involve a new (corporate) Audit Director for S, H, & E audits.
- Continuing our development in the areas of fraud detection and IT security auditing.

Internal Audit

For yet another year, we will only be able to perform priority A and B audits next year (C priority projects are considered important to the business, but without any immediate management or Audit concern.) While not atypical, at some point we need to perform audits of areas where there is no immediate concern or perceived major risk as, by definition, this is where surprises come from.

The following shows where we anticipate spending our time[118].

- Marketing, Commercial[119], and Corporate: 54%
- Refining: 39%[120]

---

[118] With so many audit engagements, it didn't make sense to put the entire list in the audit plan. However, it was available to the audit committee and each division CEO was provided a list of engagements for their division.
[119] Primarily a trading operation, including a futures and derivatives desk
[120] Rounded up

- Wood River: 8%
- Alliance: 7%
- Bayway: 6%
- Rodeo and Santa Maria: 6%
- Los Angeles: 5%
- Trainer: 3%
- Ferndale: 2%
- Ireland: 1%

Contracts Audit

On the refining side, we will be busy with several turnarounds[121], the Ferndale FCC[122], and the Bayway capital contracts.

In Phoenix, we will continue to work our way through the merchandise contracts[123] and will be heavily involved on the new building[124].

Audit Investigations

We will continue to work with management to reduce the incidence of inappropriate activities through improved systems and training. At the same time, we will continue to investigate the inevitable number of cases that are detected or reported.

Budget vs. Actual Costs

Our 2001 budget is essentially flat with the 2000 budget, allowing for the acquisitions in 2000. As in prior years, I believe this budget will

---

[121] Major maintenance that typically costs over $1 million per day.
[122] Fluid catalytic cracker, a major refinery unit that split carbon molecules using a catalyst, pressure, and heat
[123] The contracts for purchases of merchandise for our convenience stores were massive, and we recovered millions in overcharges
[124] The company was building a new HQ in Phoenix.

allow us to audit all major risks where there is value in our work. However, there are other areas that are not funded, and which will need to be audited at some point.

	TRC 2000	TRC 2001	TMC/TSS 2000	TMC/TSS 2001	Corporate 2000	Corporate 2001	TOTAL 2000	TOTAL 2001
Internal Audit	1,634	1,909	1,066	1,120	563	605	3,263	3,634
Contracts Audit	919	1,021	446	491			1,365	1,512
TOTAL	2,553	2,930	1,512	1,611	563	605	4,628	5,146

Appendix III: Business Objects Audit Plan

In 2007, the company agreed to be acquired by SAP. SAP's CFO informed us that Business Objects would be run autonomously, with integration over time. He expected that we would continue to file financial statements with the SEC in 2008, requiring Business Objects to have its own internal audit function.

The plan I submitted to the Audit Committee, shown below, had a great deal of uncertainty about how the acquisition would affect us. I was advised to assume a fully independent internal audit function, with the same responsibilities as planned before the announcement of the acquisition, changing it as required as we learned more.

INTERNAL AUDIT PLAN
2008

Introduction

Included in this document are:

1. A review of the risk assessment process followed in developing this plan
2. The results of that process, including both the risk assessment and a schedule of potential audits and reviews
3. A discussion of the plans for §404[125] project management and testing
4. A discussion of staffing and budget, with particular reference to the relationship between available resources and the work to be performed
5. An overview of the plans for the software license compliance function

---

[125] Section 404 of the Sarbanes-Oxley Act: SOX compliance

6. A brief discussion of 2008 plans for Business Contingency Planning[126]

Approvals

Approval for the following is requested from the Audit Committee:

1. The 2008 plan and budget for Internal Audit
2. The additional responsibility for coordination of Business Contingency Planning

Risk Assessment Process

As in 2007, the plan presented for 2008 is the result of a series of steps designed to identify not only those areas where there is a higher level of risk but also where audits or other work would add value to the Company.

- Norman Marks and his direct reports met through the year with members of the management team in each region and in a broad cross-section of functions.

- Based on the above, a prioritized list of potential projects (in addition to the §404[127] work), and three hi-lo risk maps (included as Attachments 1-3[128]), were prepared. These represent an internal audit perspective (as distinct from management's) on relative risks in the three areas of internal control (using the COSO definition): operational efficiency and effectiveness, compliance with applicable laws and regulations, and the integrity of financial reporting.

---

[126] Management had asked that I take on responsibility for this function because it had reported to me at previous organizations, and the audit committee was being asked to approve it – which they did.
[127] Sarbanes-Oxley §404 compliance. The SOX Coordinator reported to me, and my team performed the testing for management.
[128] Not included in this book

Auditing at the Speed of Risk with an Agile, Continuous Audit Plan

- The potential non-§404 project list and risk maps were shared with executive management, Finance leadership, and E&Y[129] for their input.
- The annual business risk assessment by management is in process. We will consider amending the plan as necessary.

2008 Priorities and Schedule of Potential Non-§404 Audits

Acknowledged best practice is for internal audit work to be aligned with business risks, which change continuously. As a result, world-class internal audit organizations develop an audit plan that is flexible, based on a continuously updated assessment of business risk.

The plan presented here is an approximation based on today's knowledge of the projects that are likely to be completed in 2008. The schedule will be updated on a regular basis.

Should the schedule of work change significantly, for example as we know more about SAP's plans, an update will be provided to the Audit Committee.

Based on the risk assessment and an assessment of the potential value of Internal Audit attention, we will select projects from this prioritized list[130].

2008 Internal Audit Projects	Priority
Change management/portfolio management (IT)	A
Continuous auditing project	A
Corporate Tax: operational audit	A
Data access and privacy (IT and PG[131])	A
Data quality and internal BI[132] (Finance and other)	A

---

[129] The external auditors
[130] The Audit Committee didn't need to see the hours for each project.
[131] The Products Development group
[132] BI refers to the internal use of the company's business analytics products.

2008 Internal Audit Projects	Priority
Director and Officer T&E[133]	A
Dublin SSC[134]: operational audit	A
E&Y financial statement audit support[135]	A
EEG/Cramer (SKO, etc.)[136]	A
Ethics Compliance and Investigations Process	A
Forecasting process	A
FP&A[137]: operational review	A
Fulfillment (operational)	A
Global Services[138] Americas (operational)	A
Global Services APJ[139] (operational)	A
Global Services EMEA[140] (operational)	A
Global transformation projects (consulting)	A
Global treasury and cash management operations	A
Greater China	A
Hedging of currency risk	A
HR practices: APJ	A
IFRS reporting and AMF filings[141]	A
India	A

---

[133] Travel and entertainment expenses of the board members and executive managers
[134] Shared Service Center
[135] EY committed to reducing fees by more than the cost of our support
[136] Events management companies. SKO was the annual Sales Kickoff Meeting, quite an extravaganza for the sales force.
[137] Financial Planning and Analysis
[138] The consulting arm of the company
[139] Asia Pacific and Japan
[140] Europe, Middle East, and Africa
[141] The company had to file with European as well as US regulators. AMF is the French regulator.

2008 Internal Audit Projects	Priority
Internal license compliance	A
Japan	A
Korea	A
Latin America - revenue and ethics	A
Management of legal expense	A
Peoplesoft HRMS[142]	A
Perimeter security (IT and PG)	A
Product development process (Product Group)	A
Recruiting from competitors[143] (Americas)	A
South Asia	A
Top-down accounting entries	A
Americas Finance workforce management	B
APJ: reconciliations of US GAAP and IFRS	B
Australia	B
Compensation practices, cost, and employee retention	B
DSO[144] management	B
Export control compliance	B
IT contingency planning	B
Local tax compliance: EMEA	B
Monthly and quarterly reporting to Corporate (Global)	B

A - high priority based on risk or value
B - 'should do' projects, time permitting
C - may do, time permitting

---

[142] Human Resources Management System
[143] This was a high risk as sometimes the new recruits brought their former company's intellectual property with them.
[144] Direct Sales Orders

Auditing at the Speed of Risk with an Agile, Continuous Audit Plan

The Plan for §404 in 2008

The work in 2007 has gone well and we anticipate additional success in 2008:

1. E&Y's reliance on our work is expected to increase further. The additional reliance they placed on Internal Audit for walkthroughs and testing resulted in significant investments in 2007 by both E&Y and Internal Audit, especially on walkthroughs performed by Internal Audit and reviewed by E&Y. We should see the benefit of that investment with reduced cost from both groups in 2008.
2. The top-down approach in 2007 will not substantially change for 2008. We will re-examine the scope based on increased materiality levels.
3. Testing will continue to be performed by Internal Audit. It will consume less than 45% of our year's resources.
4. The plan assumes that we will be required to provide an independent (from SAP) assessment of internal control over financial reporting as of 12/31/2008. We will adapt our approach if that changes.

Staffing and Budget

The budget has been built on the following assumptions:

1. The primary priority remains the testing of internal controls over financial reporting (i.e., for §404) on behalf of management. Not only is this valuable for management, but E&Y is able to place reliance on much of our work and reduce their fees.
2. Work related to §404 should be no more than 45% of the total work.
3. The work performed should be balanced, including work on risks relating to all aspects of internal control.
4. Staffing should be sufficient to perform all the high priority projects, but not necessarily any projects that are not high priority – either in terms of risk or the value to the company.

5. In addition to traditional internal audit work, the department will also provide:
    a. Leadership of the global software license compliance function
    b. §404 project leadership and management services (one person)
    c. Leadership of the Company's global risk management program
    d. Leadership and coordination of the Company's business continuation planning program (new in 2008)

The 2008 organization chart is shown below[145]. The headcount changes (subject to approval by management) are:

- The addition of a senior manager mid-2008 to lead and coordinate business continuity planning
- The addition of a senior manager in License Management[146] to assist with complex, high-value cases, and an analyst in Singapore for global letter campaigns
- The addition of an executive assistant

The budget for Internal Audit is shown below. It should be sufficient and is appropriate to the needs of the company at this time. (For the second half of 2007 and all of 2008, a separate budget has been developed for Software License Management. It is not presented here, as it is a management function and included in the Company's budget for approval by the Board.)

---

[145] It is not included in the book as it contains names.
[146] This team audited our customers for compliance with their license agreements.

	2007	2008
Payroll	1,861	2,038
Travel and Entertainment	250	274
Professional Services	207	106
Advertising and Promotions	1	
Office Expenses	31	39
Facilities	6	5
Allocation	270	296
Total Operating Expenses	2,624	2,758

Notes: 2007 includes six months' costs for the License Compliance Director. The other year-on-year variances are the result of the addition of a position mid-2008 to lead Business Continuity Planning, an assistant in early 2008, regular mid-year increases in salaries and fringe benefits, less reduced professional services costs.

Software License Compliance

This new program for 2007 has been successful, with compliance-influenced revenue through Q3 of more than $5m – an ROI in excess of 10:1. We have had successes in each geography, have a strong pipeline and management support from the top down, and anticipate an excellent Q4.

We will continue to develop the program in 2008, adding a headcount to assist with the more complex, high-value negotiations.

Business Continuity Planning

The vision for BCP is that each functional or geographic area (e.g., IT, Facilities, Employee Communications, etc.) will be responsible for developing and maintaining the response plans for their areas. However, they will follow a standard set by the new Senior Manager, who will report to the Director, Internal Controls Compliance. The Senior Manager will:

- Establish standards and templates for the BCP program, including the selection and implementation of any supporting software
- Develop and maintain the overall, highest level Executive Response Plan
- Coordinate and follow-up on progress at the detailed level
- Report to executive management on a quarterly basis

Because of potential opportunities from the SAP transaction (e.g., whether they have personnel and process we can leverage), and also due to budgetary constraints, we have deferred hiring in this area to mid-year. We will leverage existing resources to make progress in the interim, initially focusing on plans at the regional level (starting with Americas) that notify and gather executives to respond to regional crises.

About the Author

"If there were a 'Mount Rushmore' for internal audit thought leaders, Norman's likeness would be carved front and center." Richard Chambers, former President and CEO of the Institute of Internal Auditors

Norman Marks, CPA, CRMA is a (mostly) retired senior executive. He works with individuals and organizations around the world, advising them on risk management, internal audit, corporate governance, enterprise performance, and the value of information.

Norman was the chief audit executive of major global corporations for twenty years and is a globally recognized thought leader in the professions of internal auditing and risk management. In addition, he served as chief risk officer, compliance officer, and ethics officer, and led what would now be called the IT governance function (information security, contingency planning, methodologies, standards, etc.) He managed the Sarbanes-Oxley Section 404 (SOX) programs and investigation units at several companies.

He is the author of several earlier books, including:

Internal Audit

- Auditing that Matters
    - Auditing that Matters: Case Studies
    - Auditing that Matters: Case Studies Discussion Guide
- Is your Internal Audit World-Class? A Maturity Model for Internal Audit
- World-Class Internal Audit: Tales from my Journey

Risk Management

- Risk Management for Success
- Making Business Sense of Technology Risk
- Risk Management in Plain English: A Guide for Executives: Enabling Success through Intelligent and Informed Risk-Taking
- World-Class Risk Management

- World-Class Risk Management for Nonprofits (with Melanie L. Herman)

Others

- The Institute of Internal Auditors' Management's Guide to Sarbanes-Oxley Section 404: Maximize Value Within Your Organization
- How Good is your GRC? Twelve Questions to Guide Executives, Boards, and Practitioners

Norman is a retired member of the review boards of several audit and risk management publications (including the magazines of ISACA and the IIA), a frequent speaker internationally, the author of multiple award-winning articles (receiving the IIA's Thurston award in 2004 and 2014) and a prolific blogger.

Norman was profiled by the magazines of the AICPA and the IIA as an innovative and successful internal auditing leader. He has also been honored as a Fellow of the Open Compliance and Ethics Group for his GRC thought leadership, and as an Honorary Fellow of the Institute of Risk Management for his contributions to risk management. In 2018, he was inducted into the IIA's American Hall of Distinguished Practitioners.

Norman can be found at:

- Norman Marks on Governance, Risk Management, and Internal Audit
- http://twitter.com/normanmarks

Printed in Great Britain
by Amazon